# THE PASSION TRANSLATION

# Romans

## GRACE AND GLORY

Translated from Greek and Aramaic Texts

DR. BRIAN SIMMONS

tPt BIBLE

BroadStreet PUBLISHING

*Romans: Grace and Glory*
The Passion Translation®

Translated directly from the Greek and Aramaic texts by Dr. Brian Simmons

Published by BroadStreet Publishing Group, LLC
Racine, Wisconsin, USA
BroadStreetPublishing.com

© 2017 The Passion Translation®

ISBN-13: 978-1-4245-5027-2 (paperback)
ISBN-13: 978-1-4245-5028-9 (e-book)

Printed in the United States of America
17 18 19 20    10 9 8 7 6 5 4 3

# Translator's Introduction to Romans

## AT A GLANCE

*Author:* The Apostle Paul

*Audience:* The Church of Rome

*Date:* AD 55–57

*Type of Literature:* Ancient historical letter and theological essay

*Major Themes:* The gospel; salvation; the love of God; justification; God's righteousness; the law; life in the flesh vs. the Spirit; the destiny of Israel

*Outline:*

## ABOUT ROMANS

What you are about to read is a 2,000-year-old letter, penned by the apostle Paul and inspired by the Holy Spirit. You will be stirred, challenged, perhaps even corrected, as you read this enlightening letter. Paul's gospel was the gospel of grace and glory. When you receive the grace of God by faith, righteousness is birthed within your life.

The love of God is so rich; it leaves our hearts full of heaven. When we believe in Jesus Christ he pours his Holy Spirit into our hearts until every sense of abandonment leaves us. We become children of God, sons and daughters of glory, who follow the Lamb.

Do you want to be enriched and discover the heavenly treasures of faith, grace, true righteousness, and power? Plug into the book of Romans and you'll never feel the same again. Truth always sets the heart free, and nothing can free you more than the truth found in Romans. Grace and glory are waiting for you to unwrap and make your own. Live in the truths of Romans and watch how God's love sets you free!

The Protestant Reformation and the Wesleyan Revival both were born out of the revelation of righteousness found in Romans. Catch the fire of truth and grace as you read through Paul's masterpiece. While preaching in Corinth, Paul dictated the letter to Tertius (16:22) and entrusted it to Phoebe (16:1) to deliver it to the Roman believers. Phoebe was one of the outstanding women in the church of Cenchrea, a port city very near Corinth. We can date this letter to about AD 56. You can imagine the joy that came over the church at Rome when they read Paul's letter!

I encourage you to read Romans a portion at a time, first overlooking the footnotes. Then go back and make a personal study with the hundreds of study notes we have included plus the eight-week Bible study at the end of the book. You will be blessed as you read the anointed words found herein. The romance of Romans will fill you with freedom.

Freedom from sin! Freedom from self! Freedom from dead works! A new freedom is coming into your spirit as you embrace the truth of Romans!

> And you did not receive the "spirit of religious duty," leading you back into the fear of never being good enough. But you have received the "Spirit of Full Acceptance," enfolding you into the family of God. And you will never feel orphaned, for as he rises up within us, our spirits join him in saying the words of tender affection, "Beloved Father, Abba!" For the Holy Spirit makes God's fatherhood real to us as he whispers into our innermost being: "You are God's beloved child!"

> —Romans 8:15–16

## PURPOSE

Paul wrote Romans to communicate the grand themes of God's grace and glory encapsulated in the gospel! No one comes into glory except by the grace of God that fills believers with his righteousness. Our clumsy attempts to please God and the works of religion are totally unable to make us holy. But God is so kind, compassionate, and gracious that he shares his righteousness with all who receive his Son, Jesus Christ. He causes his faith-filled ones to be made holy by his grace and glory! Paul wrote his letter to clearly articulate this message, to explain why he preached it, and show how it should impact Christians in their daily life and community.

## AUTHOR AND AUDIENCE

Rome was the power center of the known world when Paul penned this letter. It was the most influential city on earth at that time. Although Paul had not yet been to Rome, he would one day be martyred there. So Paul wrote to these Roman Christians an important epistle filled with rich doctrines of our faith that reveal God's heart for his people, and what must be our proper response to such sacrificial love. Paul's theology flows from the romance of God toward us. Intimacy longs for understanding and oneness. And to be intimate with the God of glory requires that we understand his heart and join him in every way.

## MAJOR THEMES

*The Gospel.* Arguably the central focus of Paul's teaching ministry is what Christians call "the gospel." It's also the major focus of his letter to the Church of Rome, too. In the opening sentence Paul explains that God had set him apart with the mission to unveil "God's wonderful gospel" (1:1). This is one way of explaining the gospel. Here are some others: the revelation of God's Son, the wonderful message of Jesus, the joyful message of God's liberating power unleashed within us through Christ, the message of Christ's goodness, good news, and joyful news.

The Greek word for gospel is *euangelion*, which simply means "good news." Paul uses this word as shorthand for the amazing, joyful message of God's saving work in Jesus Christ. The entire Christian message is wrapped up in this one word. The gospel is the message about how God has acted in the world to rescue humanity from sin and death through the life, death, and resurrection of Jesus. So when Paul says gospel, he means all that!

*Salvation.* God's wonderful salvation is presented to us in this letter. A salvation not of works or religious efforts, but the joyous salvation that comes to everyone who believes the good news of Jesus Christ. He has come to save us and set us free. This salvation is seen in Romans as comprehensive and complete, restoring our souls to wholeness and glory, through God's endless grace.

**The Love of God.** Paul sings of God's love throughout the book of Romans! He writes that right now we "experience the endless love of God cascading into our hearts through the Holy Spirit who lives in us!" (5:5). And this love is all because of Jesus: "Christ proved God's passionate love for us by dying in our place while we were still lost and ungodly!" (5:8). If you ever doubt God's love for you, plug into Romans to be overpowered by it, realizing we will never be deprived of this gift we have in Christ Jesus!

**Justification.** One of the most powerful words Paul uses to describe our new reality in Christ is the word justified. This is a legal term that basically means "to acquit." This is God's grace at its sweetest and most potent power! While we were all at some point under God's wrath because of our sin, because Jesus paid the price of our sin in our place, we have been acquitted of all the charges against us and declared "not guilty" in heaven's courtroom!

**The Righteousness of God.** One of the most important themes of Paul in his letter to Roman Christians is righteousness, as it relates to both God and believers. He uses the word righteousness numerous times to refer to what we receive from God. Not only are we declared to be in the right, we are actually made right by God when we believe in Jesus. In fact, his righteousness is transferred to us through faith so that when we stand before God, that is who we really are: righteous!

**The Law.** Many have noted that Paul's relationship with the law is complicated, which is the Jewish law given by God to Moses for his people. In Romans, Paul says the law is "holy and its commandments are correct and for our good" (7:12). It was given to us for our benefit and intended to bring life, but instead it brought death (7:10). Paul concluded, "God achieved what the law was unable to accomplish, because the law was limited by the weakness of human nature" (8:3). Through Christ, God achieved what we could not: Christ perfectly fulfilled every requirement of the law so that now "we are free to live, not according to our flesh, but by the dynamic power of the Holy Spirit!" (8:4).

**The Flesh vs. The Spirit.** One of the most interesting comparisons Paul makes is between our old life in "the flesh" versus our new life in the "life-giving Spirit." He offers this comparison as an exhortation to live the kind of life God desires from his children—not in the morally fallen way we once lived, but in the new way as true children of God "who are moved by the impulses of the Holy Spirit" (8:14).

**The Destiny of Israel.** From the very beginning Paul makes it clear that his joyful message of what Christ has done is for every single person on the planet: "the Jew first, and then people everywhere!" (1:16). Jews and non-Jews alike are under the same curse because of sin. Paul says the same solution to that problem is available for everyone by the same faith. While the Jewish people were given this promise first, people from every nation were later "grafted in" to share in their wonderful riches. And though Jews have fallen into unbelief, Paul makes it clear God will bring all of Israel to salvation once the full number of non-Jews have come into God's family!

## A WORD ABOUT THE PASSION TRANSLATION

The message of God's story is timeless; the Word of God doesn't change. But the methods by which that story is communicated should be timely; the vessels that steward God's Word can and should change.

One of those timely methods and vessels is Bible translations. However, there is no such thing as a truly literal translation of the Bible, for there is not an equivalent language that perfectly conveys the meaning of the biblical text except as it is understood in its original cultural and linguistic setting. So it is important that a translator seeks to transfer meaning, and not merely words, from the original text to the receptor language.

The goal of The Passion Translation is to reintroduce the passion and fire of the original, life-changing message of God's Word for modern readers—not merely to convey the original, literal meaning of words, but also to express God's passion for people and his world.

God longs to have his Word expressed in every language in a way that would unlock the passion of his heart. Our goal is to trigger inside every English speaker an overwhelming response to the truth of the Bible. This is a heart-level translation, from the passion of God's heart to the passion of your heart.

We pray and trust this version of God's Word will kindle in you a burning, passionate desire for him and his heart, while impacting the church for years to come!

# One

---

¹My name is Paul, a loving and loyal servant[a] of the Anointed One, Jesus. He called me to be his apostle[b] and set me apart[c] with a mission to reveal God's wonderful gospel. I write this letter to all his beloved chosen ones in Rome, for you have been divinely summoned to be holy in his eyes.[d] May his joyous grace and total well-being, flowing from our Father and the Lord Jesus Christ, rest upon you.

²My commission is to preach the good news. Yet it is not entirely new, but the fulfillment of the hope promised to us through the many prophecies found in the sacred Scriptures.[e] ³For the gospel is all about God's Son. As a man he descended from David's royal lineage,[f] ⁴but as the mighty Son of God he was raised from the dead and miraculously

---

a 1:1 The Greek word *doulos* signifies more than a servant; it is one who has chosen to serve a master out of love, bound with cords so strong that it could only be severed by death.

b 1:1 Or "his called apostle." Paul was a servant before he was an apostle.

c 1:1 Or "permanently separated." There is an interesting wordplay here. The Aramaic word for "separated" is the root word for "Pharisee," a separated one. Paul is saying that God is the one who separated him as uniquely God's, as opposed to a self-righteous superiority. See also Galatians 1:15.

d 1:1 This sentence, although found in verse 7, has been placed here in Paul's introduction for purposes of clarity.

e 1:2 This would include the types, shadows, and prophecies of the entire Old Testament. Paul quotes from the Hebrew Scriptures (Tanakh) more than eighty times in Romans.

f 1:3 Or "the seed of David." Jesus was the "seed of the woman" in Genesis 3:15, the "seed of Abraham" in Galatians 3:16, and here in Romans 1, the "seed of David." See also Acts 13:16–41.

set apart[a] with a display of triumphant power supplied by the Spirit of Holiness.[b] And now Jesus is our Lord and our Messiah.[c] [5]Through him a joy-producing grace cascaded into us, empowering us with the gift of apostleship,[d] so that we can win people from every nation into a faithful commitment to Jesus,[e] to bring honor to his name. [6]And you are among the chosen ones who received the call to belong to Jesus, the Anointed One.[f]

## Paul's Desire to Visit Rome

[8]I give thanks to God for all of you,[g] because it's through your conversion to Jesus Christ, that the testimony of your strong, persistent faith is spreading throughout the world. [9]And God knows that I pray for you continually and at all times. For I passionately serve and worship him with my spirit through the revelation of his Son.[h]

---

a 1:4 Or "marked (appointed) as God's Son immersed in power." The Greek word for "set apart" comes from *horizo*, meaning "the horizon." It means "to mark out the boundaries, to decree, or to define." The horizon we move toward is Jesus!

b 1:4 Or "the Holy Spirit."

c 1:4 The phrase "our Lord Jesus Christ" occurs 10 times in Romans. See Acts 2:36. The word "Christ" means Anointed One.

d 1:5 Note that grace comes before service or ministry. This is likely a hendiadys: "We received the grace-gift of apostleship." See also Ephesians 4:7–13 and 1 Corinthians 15:9–10.

e 1:5 Or "the obedience of faith." The Greek text is ambiguous and can mean "the obedience to the faith" or "the obedience that springs from faith" or "the obedience that faith produces." To obey the gospel is simply to believe it!

f 1:6 Verse 7 has been merged into the text of verse 1 to enhance clarity.

g 1:8 It was Paul's constant habit to thank God for any grace he found within any believer.

h 1:9 As translated from the Aramaic. The Greek is "whom I serve in my spirit in the gospel."

¹⁰My desire and constant prayer is that I would be able to come and visit you,ᵃ according to the plan and timing of God.ᵇ ¹¹I yearn to come and be face-to-face with you and get to know you. For I long to impart to youᶜ the gift of the Spiritᵈ that will empower you to stand strong in your faith. ¹²Now, this means that when we come together and are side by side, something wonderful will be released. We can expect to be co-encouraged and co-comforted by each other's faith!

⇠¹³So, my dear brothers and sisters, please don't interpret my failure to visit you as indifference, because many times I've intended to come but have not been releasedᵉ to do so up to now. For I long to enjoy a harvest of spiritual fruitᶠ among you, like I have experienced among the nations. ¹⁴Love obligates me to preach to everyone, to those who are among the elite and those who are among the outcasts,ᵍ to those who are wise and educated as well as to those who are foolish and

---

ₐ 1:10 As translated from the Aramaic. The Greek is "that I may have a smooth and prosperous journey to you." But in fact, Paul had a very difficult journey to Rome, first traveling by ship, enduring a shipwreck, and being bitten by a snake. See Acts 27–28. One can only imagine what would have happened if Paul had not prayed for a smooth and prosperous journey!

ᵦ 1:10 Or "as God prospers me along the path of his will."

ᵪ 1:11 Or "share with you."

ᵨ 1:11 As translated from the Aramaic. The Greek is "a spiritual gift." See also Romans 15:29.

ₑ 1:13 Or "have been hindered (due to missionary work)." There is no implication that the Devil hindered Paul from coming, but rather, the missionary work of ministering in Turkey (Asia Minor).

ᵩ 1:13 This "fruit" would imply both converts and bringing the believers into maturity.

₉ 1:14 Or "to the Greek speakers and to the barbarians." By implication, Paul is obligated by love to preach to the cultured Greek speakers and to those who are uncultured foreigners.

unlearned. [15]This is why I am so excited[a] about coming to preach the wonderful message of Jesus[b] to you in Rome!

## The Gospel of Power

[16]I refuse to be ashamed of sharing the wonderful message of God's liberating power unleashed in us through Christ! For I am thrilled to preach that everyone who believes is saved—the Jew first,[c] and then people everywhere! [17]This gospel unveils a continual revelation of God's righteousness—a perfect righteousness given to us when we believe.[d] And it moves us from receiving life through faith, to the power of living by faith.[e] This is what the Scripture means when it says:

---

[a] 1:15 Or "To my very uttermost I am eager."

[b] 1:15 Or "good news (gospel)" or "message of goodness (well-being)."

[c] 1:16 Salvation comes to us through the Jewish people in our Lord Jesus Christ. The promised salvation message came historically to the Jew first, but by priority and privilege our obligation of love continues to bring the sweet message of Yeshua's grace to our Jewish friends.

[d] 1:17 Implied in the immediate context. Although the full meaning of the Greek words *dikaiosynē theou* is greatly debated, this refers to the power of the gospel that imparts to believers God's righteousness. This is the justifying power that comes through faith. The word *of* (righteousness of God) is a genitive of source or cause. It is the righteousness *from* God coming into us who believe. See 2 Corinthians 5:21, where *dikaiosynē theou* is also found. However, to insist that the gospel be preached in this day first to the Jew is to deny the truth that there is no distinction between Jew and Gentile. See Galatians 4:12 and Romans 3:22.

[e] 1:17 Ancient expositors taught that we move from what we once believed in to believing in God alone for righteousness. For the Jew it means moving from faith in Torah and doing well to a faith in the works of Yeshua, the Living Torah, who alone brings us into salvation's power. For those in any religion, it means moving from an impotent faith into the explosive faith of the gospel of Christ.

**"We are right with God through life-giving faith!"**[a]

## God Reveals His Wrath

[18]For God in heaven unveils his holy anger[b] breaking forth against every form of sin, both toward ungodliness that lives in hearts and evil actions. For the wickedness of humanity deliberately smothers the truth and keeps people from acknowledging the truth about God. [19]In reality, the truth of God is known instinctively,[c] for God has embedded this knowledge inside every human heart. [20]Opposition to truth cannot be excused on the basis of ignorance,[d] because from the creation of the world, the invisible qualities[e] of God's nature have been made visible, such as his eternal power and transcendence. He has made his wonderful attributes easily perceived,[f] for seeing the visible makes us understand the invisible.[g] So then, this leaves everyone without excuse.

[21]*Throughout human history*[h] the fingerprints of God were upon

---

a  1:17 Or "It is through faith that the righteous enter into life (salvation)." See Habakkuk 2:4.

b  1:18 Or "wrath." God's wrath is his action in punishing evil, a holy disapproval of all that is seen as wicked in the eyes of his holiness. In this first chapter, both righteousness and wrath are revealed. Righteousness is revealed in the gospel, but wrath is revealed as an activity God takes to uphold his glory.

c  1:19 Or "The knowability of God is manifest in them."

d  1:20 Implied by the immediate context and by the use of the conjunction *because*. This form of ellipsis needs to be supplied for the sake of clarity.

e  1:20 The Aramaic is "his holy attributes."

f  1:20 Or "lies plainly before their eyes." The literal Greek is "being intellectually apprehended by reflection."

g  1:20 That is, what the eye sees becomes revelation to the conscience. See Psalm 19:1–4.

h  1:21 This phrase is implied by the use of the Greek aorist verb tense and is important for clarity as Paul continues to describe the brokenness of fallen humanity.

them,[a] yet they refused to honor him as God or even be thankful for his kindness. Instead, they entertained corrupt and foolish thoughts about what God was like.[b] This left them with nothing but misguided hearts, steeped in moral darkness. ²²Although claiming to be super-intelligent,[c] they were in fact shallow fools.[d] ²³For only a fool would trade the unfading splendor of the immortal God to worship the fading image of other humans, idols made to look like people, animals, birds, and even creeping reptiles!

²⁴This is why God lifted off his restraining hand and let them have full expression of their sinful and shameful desires. They were given over to moral depravity, dishonoring their bodies *by sexual perversion*[e] among themselves—²⁵all because they traded the truth of God for a lie.[f] They worshiped and served the things God made rather than the God who made all things—glory and praises to him for eternity of eternities![g] Amen!

²⁶⁻²⁷For this reason God gave them over to their own disgraceful and vile passions.[h] Enflamed with lust for one another, men and women ignored the natural order and exchanged normal sexual relations for homosexuality. Women engaged in lesbian conduct, and men

---

a 1:21 Or "They instinctively knew (there was a) God."
b 1:21 Or "They became futile in their reasoning."
c 1:22 Or "wise."
d 1:22 The Aramaic is "They became insane."
e 1:24 Implied in the text.
f 1:25 An obvious metonymy, equating an idol with "a lie." See 2 Thessalonians 2:11.
g 1:25 As translated from the Aramaic.
h 1:26-27 The Aramaic is "disgraceful diseases."

committed shameful acts with men,[a] receiving in themselves the due penalty for their deviation.[b]

28And because they thought it was worthless to embrace the true knowledge of God, God gave them over[c] to a worthless mind-set, to break all rules of proper conduct. 29Their sinful lives became full of every kind of evil,[d] wicked schemes,[e] greed,[f] and cruelty. Their hearts overflowed with jealous cravings, and with conflict and strife, which drove them into hateful arguments and murder. They are deceitful liars full of hostility. They are gossips 30who love to spread malicious slander. With inflated egos they hurl hateful insults at God, yet they are nothing more than arrogant boasters. They are rebels against their parents and totally immoral. 31They are senseless, faithless,[g] ruthless, heartless, and completely merciless.[h] 32Although they are fully aware of God's laws and proper order, and knowing that those who do all of these things deserve to die, yet they still go headlong into darkness, encouraging others to do the same and applauding them when they do!

---

a 1:26-27 See Leviticus 18:22.

b 1:26-27 Some see an inference here to sexually transmitted diseases.

c 1:28 This is the third time that it states, "God gave them over." See vs. 24, 26–27, and here in v. 28.

d 1:29 There are 22 Greek nouns and adjectives used for evil listed in v. 29–32. Injustice (selfishness), destructiveness, covetousness, malice, envy, murder, strife, guile, hostility, slander (the hissing sound of a snake charmer), gossip, hateful to God, insolent, arrogant, disobedient to parents, without moral understanding, without faith, without natural affections, hostilities, without mercy.

e 1:29 The Aramaic and some Greek manuscripts have "immorality."

f 1:29 Or "unrestrained selfishness."

g 1:31 Or "covenant-breakers."

h 1:31 The Aramaic renders this verse "They have no stability in themselves, neither love, nor peace, nor compassion."

*Two*

## God Judges Sin

[1]No matter who you are, before you judge the wickedness of others, you had better remember this: you are also without excuse, for you too are guilty of the same kind of things! When you judge others, and then do the same things they do, you condemn yourself.[a] [2]We know that God's judgment falls upon those who practice these things. God is always right, because he has all the facts.[b] [3]And no matter who you think you are, when you judge others who do these things and then do the same things yourself, what makes you think that you will escape God's judgment?

[4]Do the riches of his extraordinary kindness make you take him for granted and despise him? Haven't you experienced how kind and understanding he has been to you? Don't mistake his tolerance for acceptance. Do you realize that all the wealth of his extravagant kindness[c] is meant to melt your heart and lead you into repentance?[d] [5]But because of your calloused heart and refusal to change direction, you are piling up wrath for yourself in the day of wrath, when God's righteous judgment is revealed.

---

a 2:1 The Aramaic reads, "Because of this, O human, the Spirit is not speaking through you as you judge another, for against what you judge, you will also revert."

b 2:2 Or "It (judgment) is based on truth."

c 2:4 The Aramaic word for kindness is actually "sweetness."

d 2:4 The Aramaic reads, "Do you now know that it is the fulfillment of God to bring you blessings?"

⁶For:

**He will give to each one in return for what he has done.**[a]

⁷For those living in constant goodness and doing what pleases him,[b] seeking an unfading glory and honor and imperishable virtue, will experience eternal life. ⁸But those governed by selfishness and self-promotion, whose hearts are unresponsive to God's truth and would rather embrace unrighteousness, will experience the fullness of wrath.[c]

⁹Anyone who does evil can expect tribulation and distress—to the Jew first and also to the non-Jew. ¹⁰But when we do what pleases God, we can expect unfading glory, true honor, and a continual peace—to the Jew first and also to the non-Jew, ¹¹for God sees us all without partiality.

¹²When people who have never been exposed to the laws of Moses commit sin, they will still perish for what they do. And those who are under the law of Moses and fail to obey it are condemned by the law. ¹³For it's not merely knowing the law[d] that makes you right with God, but doing all that the law says that will cause God to pronounce you innocent.[e]

---

a 2:6 See Psalm 62:12, Proverbs 24:12, and Matthew 16:27.

b 2:7 Doing what pleases God comes from faith. We must first believe in Jesus, the Anointed One. Then our life and works will bring honor to him. See also verse 10, John 6:28–29, and Hebrews 11:6

c 2:8 God's wrath is mentioned twelve times in Romans (1:18, 2:5, 2:8, 3:5, 4:15, 5:9, 9:22, 12:19, 13:4, and 13:5).

d 2:13 Every Sabbath day the Mosaic law, the Torah, was read in the Jewish meeting house.

e 2:13 Or "righteous." See Deuteronomy 18:5. No one keeps the law in every part; this is why Yeshua (Jesus) came to redeem and save us. See also Romans 3:20.

## God's Judgment

[14]For example, whenever people who don't possess the law[a] as their birthright commit sin, it still confirms that a "law" is present in their conscience. For when they instinctively do what the law requires, that becomes a "law" to govern them, even though they don't have Mosaic law. [15]It demonstrates that the requirements of the law are woven into their hearts. They know what is right and wrong, for their conscience validates this "law" in their heart. Their thoughts correct[b] them in one instance and commend them in another. [16]So this judgment will be revealed on the day when God, through Jesus the Messiah, judges the hidden secrets of people's hearts. And their response to the gospel I preach will be the standard of judgment used in that day.

## The Jewish Religion Will Not Save You

[17]Now, you claim to be a Jew because you lean upon your trust in the law[c] and boast in your relationship with God. [18]And you claim to know the will of God, and to have the moral high ground because you've been taught the law of Moses. [19]You are also confident that you are a qualified guide to those who are "blind," a shining light to those who live in darkness. [20]You are confident that you are a true teacher of the foolish and immature,[d] all because you have the treasury of truth and knowledge in the law of Moses. [21]So let me ask you this: Why don't you practice what you preach? You preach, "Don't steal!" but are you a thief? [22]You are swift to tell others, "Don't commit adultery!" but are you guilty of adultery? You say, "I hate idolatry and false gods!" but do you

---

a 2:14 Or "Torah (the first five books of Moses)."

b 2:15 Or "accuse."

c 2:17 The Aramaic is "You take comfort from the law."

d 2:20 Or "little children," a metaphor for the untutored or the immature.

withhold from the true God what is due him?[a] 23Even though you boast in the law, you dishonor God, the Lawgiver, when you break it! 24For your actions seem to fulfill what is written:

**"God's precious name is cursed among the nations because of you."**[b]

25You trust in the covenant sign of circumcision,[c] yet circumcision only has value if you faithfully keep the teachings of the law. But if you violate the law, you have invalidated your circumcision.[d] 26And if the uncircumcised one faithfully keeps the law, won't his obedience make him more "Jewish" than the actual rite of circumcision? 27And won't the one who has never had the knife cut his foreskin be your judge when you break the law? 28You are not a Jew if it's only superficial—for it's more than the surgical cut of a knife that makes you Jewish. 29But you are Jewish because of the inward act of spiritual circumcision—a radical change that lays bare your heart. It's not by the principle of law,[e] but by power of the Holy Spirit. For then your praise will not come from people, but from God himself!

---

a 2:22 Or "Do you rob temples?" The Aramaic is "You plunder the Holy Place."

b 2:24 See LXX Isaiah 52:5 and Ezekiel 36:20.

c 2:25 Implied by the immediate context and by the use of the conjunction *for*. This form of ellipsis needs to be supplied for the sake of clarity.

d 2:25 Or "Your circumcision has become uncircumcision."

e 2:29 Or "by the letter."

## Three

## God's Righteousness

¹So then what is the importance of circumcision, and what advantage is there of being a Jew? ²Actually, there are numerous advantages.ª Most important, God *distinguished the Jews from all other people*ᵇ by entrusting them with the revelation of his prophetic promises.ᶜ ³But what if some were unfaithful to their divine calling? Does their unbelief weaken God's faithfulness? ⁴Absolutely not! God will always be proven faithful and true to his word, while people are proven to be liars. This will fulfill what was written in the Scriptures:

> **Your words will always be vindicated**
> **and you will rise victorious**
> **when you are being tried by your critics!**ᵈ

⁵But what if our wrong shows how right God is? Doesn't our bad serve the purpose of making God look good? (Of course, I'm only speaking from a human viewpoint.) Would that infer that God is unfair when he displays his anger against wrongdoing? ⁶Absolutely not! For if that were the case, how could God be the righteous judge of all the earth?

---

a 3:2 The Aramaic can be translated "They have increased (prospered) in every way."

b 3:2 Implied in the context.

c 3:2 These prophetic messages ("messages," "oracles," or "sayings") include the entire scope of revelation given to the Jews through the teachings of the Torah and the many prophecies of the coming Messiah, all finding their fulfillment in Jesus, the Anointed One.

d 3:4 Or "You will prevail when judged." See Psalm 51:4.

⁷So, if my lie brings into sharp contrast the brightness of God's truth, and if my lie accentuates his glory, then why should I be condemned as a sinner? ⁸Is it proper for us to sin, just so we can be forgiven?ᵃ May it never be! Yet there are some who slander us and claim that is what we teach. They deserve to be condemned for even saying it!

## Universal Sinfulness

⁹So, are we to conclude then that we Jews are superior to all others? Certainly not! For we have already provenᵇ that both Jews and Gentiles are all under the bondage of sin. ¹⁰And the Scriptures agree, for it is written:

> **There is no one who always does what is right,**
> > **no, not even one!**
> ¹¹**There is no one with true spiritual insight.**
> > **and there is no one who seeks after God alone.**
> ¹²**All have deliberately wandered from God's ways.**
> > **All have become depraved and unfit.**
> > **Kindness has disappeared from them all,**
> > **not even one is good.**ᶜ
> ¹³**Their words release a stench,**ᵈ
> > **like the smell of death—foul and filthy!**ᵉ
> > **Deceitful lies roll off their tongues.**
> > **The venom of a viper drips from their lips.**ᶠ

---

ᵃ 3:8 As translated from the Aramaic and implied in the Greek, which reads, "to do evil so that good may come."

ᵇ 3:9 Or "accused" or "drawn up an indictment."

ᶜ 3:12 This is quoted from the Greek LXX of Psalm 14:1–3 and 53:3.

ᵈ 3:13 Or "Their throats are open graves," a metonymy for their speech.

ᵉ 3:13 See Psalm 5:9.

ᶠ 3:13 See Psalm 140:3.

[14]Bitter profanity flows from their mouths,
only meant to cut and harm.[a]
[15]They are infatuated with violence and murder.[b]
[16]They release ruin and misery wherever they go.
[17]They never experience the path of peace.[c]
[18]They shut their eyes to the awe-inspiring God![d]

[19]Now, we realize that everything the law says is addressed to those who are under its authority. This is for two reasons: So that every excuse will be silenced, *with no boasting of innocence.*[e] And so that the entire world will be held accountable to God's standards.[f] [20]For by the merit of observing the law no one earns the status of being declared righteous before God, for it is the law that fully exposes and unmasks the reality of sin.

## The Gospel Reveals God's Righteousness

[21-22]But now, independently of the law, the righteousness of God is tangible and brought to light through Jesus, the Anointed One. This is the righteousness that the Scriptures prophesied would come.[g] It is God's righteousness made visible through the faithfulness of Jesus Christ.[h] And now all who believe in him receive that gift. For there is really no difference between us, [23]for we all have sinned and are in need of the glory

---

a 3:14 See Psalm 10:7.

b 3:15 Or "Their feet are swift to shed blood."

c 3:17 Verses 15–17 are quoted from Isaiah 59:7–8.

d 3:18 See Psalm 36:1. Paul lists a total of fourteen truths that describe all of humanity from the Old Testament.

e 3:19 Implied in the context. "Every mouth will be silenced" means that there will be no one boasting that they are innocent before God.

f 3:19 Or "may be liable to judgment by God."

g 3:21-22 Or "attested to by the Law and the Prophets."

h 3:21-22 Or "through faith in Jesus Christ."

of God. [24]Yet through his powerful declaration of acquittal, God freely gives away his righteousness. His gift[a] of love and favor now cascades over us, all because Jesus, the Anointed One, has liberated us from *the guilt, punishment, and power of* sin!

[25]Jesus' God-given destiny[b] was to be the sacrifice to take away sins, and now he is our Mercy Seat[c] because of his death on the cross. We come to him for mercy, for God has made a provision for us to be forgiven by faith in the sacred blood of Jesus. This is the perfect demonstration of God's justice, because until now, he had been so patient—holding back his justice out of his tolerance for us. So he covered over[d] the sins of those who lived prior to Jesus' sacrifice. [26]And when the season of tolerance came to an end, there was only one possible way for God to give away his righteousness and still be true to both his justice and his mercy—to offer up his own Son. So now, because we stand on the faithfulness of Jesus,[e] God declares us righteous in his eyes!

[27]Where, then, is there room for boasting? Do our works bring God's acceptance? Not at all! It was not our works of keeping the law

---

a  3:24 The Greek word is *dorean,* which means "present, gift, legacy, privilege."
b  3:25 The Aramaic is "God ordained in advance an atonement by faith in his (Jesus') blood."
c  3:25 Or "propitiation." The *mercy seat* becomes a metonymy for the sacrificial, redemptive work of Christ. The mercy seat was the lid to the ark of the covenant, which was carried throughout the wilderness for years and finally found a home in the temple in Jerusalem. "Blood of mercy" was sprinkled on the mercy seat (or "place of satisfaction") yearly on the Day of Atonement, which covered the sins of the people until Jesus sprinkled his blood on the mercy seat in the heavens. The mercy seat was not seen by the people; only the high priest went into the Holy of Holies to sprinkle blood upon the mercy seat. Yet Jesus was publicly offered as the satisfaction for sin's consequences.
d  3:25 Or "passed over, released (let it be)." This is the only place the Greek word *paresis* is found in the New Testament.
e  3:26 Or "faith in Jesus."

but our faith[a] in his finished work *that makes us right with God.* [28]So our conclusion is this: God's wonderful declaration that we are righteous[b] in his eyes can only come when we put our faith in Christ, and not in keeping the law.

## The God of all the People

[29]After all, is God the God of the Jews only, or is he equally the God for all of humanity? Of course, he's the God of all people! [30]Since there is only one God, he will treat us all the same—he eliminates our guilt and makes us right with him by faith no matter who we are.[c] [31]Does emphasizing our faith invalidate the law? Absolutely not. Instead, our faith establishes the role the law should rightfully have.[d]

---

a 3:27 The Aramaic reads, "It was not our works of keeping Torah, but the Torah of faith." The Greek is "the law (principle) of faith."

b 3:28 Or "continually made righteous."

c 3:30 Or "whether they are circumcised or uncircumcised."

d 3:31 Or "upholds the law." The rightful role of the law is to bring conviction of sin (3:19–20) and to present God's standard of holiness, now fulfilled in Christ (8:4).

# Four

## Abraham's Faith

[1]Let me use Abraham as an example. It is clear that humanly speaking, he was the founder of Judaism. What was his experience of being made right with God? [2]Was it by his good works of keeping the law? No. For if it was by the things he did, he would have something to boast about, but no one boasts before God. [3]Listen to what the Scriptures say:

> **Because Abraham believed God's words, his faith transferred God's righteousness into his account.**[a]

[4]When people work, they earn wages. It can't be considered a free gift, because they earned it. [5]But no one earns God's righteousness. It can only be transferred when we no longer rely on our own works, but believe in the one who powerfully declares the ungodly to be righteous[b] in his eyes. It is faith that transfers God's righteousness into your account!

## David's Faith

[6]Even King David himself speaks to us regarding the complete wholeness that comes inside a person when God's powerful declaration of righteousness is heard over our life. Apart from our works, God's work is enough. [7]Here's what David says:

---

a 4:3 See Genesis 15:6.

b 4:5 Or "calculated (reckoned) to be righteous." The Greek word *logizomai* is used eleven times in this chapter. This teaches us that our faith is considered or calculated as righteousness before God.

> **What happy fulfillment is ahead for those**[a]
> **whose rebellion has been forgiven**
> **and whose sins are covered by blood.**[b]
> **⁸What happy progress comes to them**
> **when they hear the Lord speak over them,**
> **"I will never hold your sins against you!"**[c]

⁹Now, think about it. Does this happiness come only to the Jews, or is it available to all who believe?[d] Our answer is this: faith was credited to Abraham as God's righteousness![e]

¹⁰How did he receive this gift of righteousness? Was he circumcised at the time God accepted him, or was he still uncircumcised? Clearly, he was an uncircumcised Gentile when God said this of him! ¹¹It was later that he received the external sign of circumcision as a seal to confirm that God had already transferred his righteousness to him by faith, while he was still uncircumcised. So now this qualifies him to become the father of all who believe among the non-Jewish people. And like their "father of faith," Abraham, God also transfers his righteousness to them by faith. ¹²Yes, Abraham is obviously the true father of faith for the

---

a  4:7 See Psalm 32:1. The Hebrew word for "blessed" or "happy" is *asher*, which carries the meaning of "a happy progress." See also verse 8.

b  4:7 Implied in the context. When David wrote this Psalm, it was during the days of covering sin by the blood of sacrifice. Today our sins are no longer covered, but removed forever.

c  4:8 The Greek uses the word *logizomai*, which means to take an inventory and settle accounts. God has taken inventory of the virtue of Christ, and through our faith in him, his perfect righteousness is now deposited in our account. It is settled; we are declared righteous by faith.

d  4:9 Or "Is this happiness then for those who are the circumcision or also for the uncircumcision?"

e  4:9 See Genesis 15:6.

Jewish people who are not only circumcised but who walk in the way of faith that our father Abraham displayed before his circumcision.

## The Promise of Faith versus Keeping the Law

¹³God promised Abraham and his descendants that they would have an heir who would reign over the world.ᵃ This royal promise was not fulfilled because Abraham kept all the law, but through the righteousness that was transferred by faith. ¹⁴For if keeping the law earns the inheritance, then faith is robbed of its power and the promise becomes useless. ¹⁵For the law provokes punishment, and where no law exists there cannot be a violation of the law.

¹⁶The promise depends on faith so that it can be experienced as a grace-gift, and now it extends to all the descendants of Abraham. This promise is not only meant for those who obey the law, but also to those who enter into the faith of Abraham, the father of us all. ¹⁷That's what the Scripture means when it says:

**"I have made you the father of many nations."**ᵇ

He is our example and father, for in God's presence he believed that God can raise the dead and call into being things that don't even exist yet.ᶜ ¹⁸Against all odds, when it looked hopeless, Abraham believed the

---

ᵃ 4:13 As translated from the Aramaic. The Greek is "for the promise made to Abraham or to his descendants that he would inherit the world," and is somewhat confusing since there is no promise in Scripture that Abraham would inherit "the whole world." This is an obvious statement about Abraham's heir Jesus Christ, who is given the dominion over the whole world.

ᵇ 4:17 See Genesis 17:5.

ᶜ 4:17 This is perfectly illustrated with God speaking to Abraham about nations coming from him and his wife even though they had no children and were beyond the age of childbearing. The God who creates out of nothing could give children and eventually nations to Abraham and Sarah.

promise and expected God to fulfill it.[a] He took God at his word, and as a result he became the father of many nations. God's declaration over him came to pass:

> **"Your descendants will be so many**
> **that they will be impossible to count!"[b]**

[19]In spite of being nearly one hundred years old when the promise of having a son was made, his faith was so strong that it could not be undermined by the fact that he and Sarah[c] were incapable of conceiving a child. [20-21]He never stopped believing God's promise, for he was made strong in his faith[d] *to father a child.* And because he was mighty in faith and convinced that God had all the power needed to fulfill his promises, Abraham glorified God!

[22]So now you can see why Abraham's faith was credited to his account as righteousness before God.[e] [23]And this declaration was not just spoken over Abraham, [24]but also over us. For when we believe and embrace the one who brought our Lord Jesus back to life, perfect righteousness will be credited to our account as well. [25]Jesus was handed over to be crucified for the forgiveness of our sins and was raised back to life to prove that he had made us right with God![f]

---

a 4:18 Or "who beyond hope in hope believed."

b 4:18 See Genesis 15:5. Although only a portion of Genesis 15:5 is quoted here, the entire text is implied here and is supplied to bring clarity to the English narrative.

c 4:19 Or "and the deadness of Sarah's womb."

d 4:20-21 Or "He was empowered in faith."

e 4:22 See Genesis 15:6.

f 4:25 In this poetic verse we discover that the blood of the cross is the means of our justification and the resurrection is the proof that God now sees believers as righteous in his eyes.

## *Five*
—

### Our New Life

[1]Our faith in Jesus transfers God's righteousness to us and he now declares us flawless in his eyes.[a] This means we can now enjoy true and lasting peace[b] with God, all because of what our Lord Jesus, the Anointed One, has done for us. [2]Our faith guarantees us permanent access into this marvelous kindness[c] that has given us a perfect relationship with God. What incredible joy bursts forth within us as we keep on celebrating our hope of experiencing God's glory!

[3]But that's not all! Even in times of trouble we have a joyful confidence, knowing that our pressures will develop in us patient endurance. [4]And patient endurance will refine our character, and proven character leads us back to hope. [5]And this hope is not a disappointing fantasy,[d] because we can now experience the endless love of God cascading into our hearts through the Holy Spirit who lives in us![e]

[6]For when the time was right, the Anointed One came and died *to demonstrate his love*[f] for sinners who were entirely helpless, weak, and powerless to save themselves.

---

a  5:1 Or "having already been declared righteous." What bliss! We are declared righteous in the eyes of the Holy God. This is the wonder of grace!

b  5:1 Or "Let us enjoy peace with God." The Greek word for peace is *eirene* and can also mean "to join (as in a dove-tail joint)." We have entered into the union of our lives with God's peace and enjoy lasting friendship with God. The Hebrew word is *shalom*, which means abundant peace and well-being.

c  5:2 Or "grace."

d  5:5 Or "This hope does not put one to shame."

e  5:5 Or "was given to us."

f  5:6 Implied both in the text and the context.

[7]Now, who of us would dare to die for the sake of a wicked person?[a] We can all understand if someone was willing to die for a truly noble person. [8]But Christ proved God's passionate love for us by dying in our place while we were still lost and ungodly!

[9]And there is still much more to say of his unfailing love for us! For through the blood of Jesus we have heard the powerful declaration, "You are now righteous in my sight." And because of the sacrifice of Jesus, you will never experience the wrath of God. [10]So if while we were still enemies, God fully reconciled[b] us to himself through the death of his Son, then something greater than friendship is ours. Now that we are at peace with God, and because we share in his resurrection life, how much more we will be rescued from sin's dominion![c]

[11]And even more than that, we overflow with triumphant joy[d] in our new relationship of living in harmony[e] with God—all because of Jesus Christ!

## The Gift of Grace Greater than Sin

[12]When Adam sinned, the entire world was affected. Sin entered human experience, and death was the result. And so death followed this sin,[f] casting its shadow over all humanity, because all have sinned. [13]Sin was

---

a 5:7 As translated from the Aramaic. The Greek reads, "Rarely would anyone die for a righteous person."

b 5:10 The Greek verb for reconciled is actually "exchanged." That is, he exchanged our sins for his righteousness and thus reconciled us to God. The reign of death is caused by the guilt of sin.

c 5:10 Although implied, the life by which Jesus saves us is resurrection life. See also John 14:19 and Hebrews 7:25.

d 5:11 Or "boasting (in God)."

e 5:11 As translated from the Aramaic, which can also be translated "By him (Jesus) we now accept his door-opening." The Greek is "reconciled."

f 5:12 "This sin" is translated from the Aramaic.

in the world before Moses gave the written law, but it was not charged against them where no law existed.[a] 14Yet death reigned[b] as king from Adam to Moses even though they hadn't broken a command the way Adam had.[c] The first man, Adam, was a picture[d] of the Messiah, who was to come.[e]

15Now, there is no comparison between Adam's transgression and the gracious gift that we experience. *For the magnitude of the gift far outweighs the crime.*[f] It's true that many died because of one man's transgression, but how much greater will God's grace and his gracious gift of acceptance overflow[g] to many because of what one Man, Jesus, the Messiah, did for us!

16And this free-flowing gift imparts to us much more than what was given to us through the one who sinned. For because of one transgression, we are all facing a death sentence with a verdict of "Guilty!" But this gracious gift leaves us free from our many failures[h] and brings us into the perfect righteousness of God—acquitted with the words "Not guilty!"

---

a 5:13 That is, there was no ability to be charged and found guilty of breaking the law.

b 5:14 Death is a temporary monarch that exercises dominion over humanity, but one day it will be completely deposed and defeated through Jesus Christ.

c 5:14 Implied in the text and in the meaning of the word *transgressed.*

d 5:14 Or "imprint."

e 5:14 The actions of both Adam and Christ affect the entire world. Death passes to all who are in Adam; life passes to all who are in Christ. Each is a corporate head of a race of people. God sees every person as in Adam or in Christ.

f 5:15 Although clearly implied in the text, this summary of explanation is important as it makes explicit Paul's contrast between Adam's transgression and Christ's redemption.

g 5:15 Or "multiply" or "super-abound."

h 5:16 Or "falls," or "trespasses."

[17]Death once held us in its grip, and by the blunder of one man, death reigned as king over humanity. But now, how much more[a] are we held in the grip of grace and continue reigning as kings in life, enjoying our regal freedom through the gift of perfect righteousness[b] in the one and only Jesus, the Messiah!

[18]In other words, just as condemnation came upon all people through one transgression, so through one righteous act *of Jesus' sacrifice*, the perfect righteousness that makes us right with God and leads us to a victorious life[c] is now available to all. [19]One man's disobedience opened the door for all humanity to become sinners. So also one man's obedience opened the door for many to be made perfectly right with God and acceptable to him. [20]So then, the law was introduced into God's plan to bring the reality of human sinfulness out of hiding. And yet, wherever sin increased, there was more than enough of God's grace to triumph all the more![d] [21]And just as sin reigned through death, so also this sin-conquering grace will reign as king through righteousness, imparting eternal life through Jesus, our Lord and Messiah!

---

[a] 5:17 There are four "much mores" in this chapter. Two point to our future deliverance (v. 9 and 10), and two point to the abundance of grace which we now experience (v. 15 and 17).

[b] 5:17 Or "the gift of covenant membership."

[c] 5:18 As translated from the Aramaic. The Greek is "which brings righteousness of life."

[d] 5:20 Paul speaks of God's grace in verse 17 as super-abundant, but then adds the prefix, "huper (hyper)" making grace *huperperisseuō*, which could be translated super-hyper-abundant grace! There is an endless fountain of grace that has been opened for us in Christ!

*Six*

## The Triumph of Grace over Sin

¹So what do we do, then? Do we persist in sin so that God's kindness and grace will increase? ²What a terrible thought! We have died to sin once and for all, as a dead man passes away from this life. So how could we live under sin's rule a moment longer? ³Or have you forgotten that all of us who were immersed into union with Jesus, the Anointed One, were immersed into union with his death?

⁴Sharing in his death by our baptism means that we were co-buried and entombed with him, so that when the Father's glory raised Christ from the dead, we were also raised with him. We have been co-resurrected with him so that we could be empowered to walk in the freshness of new life. ⁵For since we are permanently grafted into him[a] to experience a death like his, then we are permanently grafted into him to experience a resurrection like his and the new life that it imparts.

⁶Could it be any clearer[b] that our former identity[c] is now and forever deprived of its power? For we were co-crucified with him to dismantle the stronghold of sin within us,[d] so that we would not continue to live one moment longer submitted to sin's power.[e]

---

a 6:5 Or "if we have become grown-together as one with him."

b 6:6 Or "Coming to know this," or "Coming to the realization."

c 6:6 The Aramaic is "our old son of Adam."

d 6:6 Or "body of sin would no longer have dominion over us."

e 6:6 Or "that the body of sin might be annulled (put out of business)." To beg God for victory over sin is a refusal to understand that we have already died to sin. Our joyful task is to believe the good news, rather than to seek to "crucify ourselves." Sin is not suppressed by the cross; it is eliminated. Upon this "water" God commands us to step out and walk upon it, for we are now in him.

[7]Obviously, a dead person is incapable of sinning. [8]And if we were co-crucified with the Anointed One, we know that we will also share in the fullness of his life. [9]And we know that since the Anointed One has been raised from the dead to die no more, his resurrection life has vanquished death and its power over him is finished. [10]For by his sacrifice he died to sin's power once and for all,[a] but he now lives continuously for the Father's pleasure. [11]So let it be the same way with you! Since you are now joined with him, you must continually view yourselves as dead and unresponsive to sin's appeal while living daily for God's pleasure in union with Jesus, the Anointed One.

## Sin's Reign Is Over

[12]Sin is a dethroned monarch; so you must no longer give it an opportunity to rule over your life, controlling how you live and compelling you to obey its desires and cravings. [13]So then, refuse to answer its call to surrender your body as a tool for wickedness. Instead, passionately answer God's call to keep yielding your body to him as one who has now experienced resurrection life! You live now for his pleasure, ready to be used for his noble purpose.[b] [14]Remember this: sin will not conquer you, for God already has! You are not governed by law but governed by the reign of the grace of God.

## Grace Frees Us to Serve God

[15]What are we to do, then? Should we sin to our hearts' content since there's no law to condemn us anymore? What a terrible thought! [16]Don't you realize that grace frees you to choose your own master? But choose carefully, for you surrender yourself to become a servant—bound to the

---

a 6:10 See also Hebrews 9:26–28.

b 6:13 Or "For the members of your body will be used as weapons for the righteousness of God."

one you choose to obey. If you choose to love sin, it will become your master, and it will own you and reward you with death. But if you choose to love and obey God, he will lead you into perfect righteousness.

[17]And God is pleased with you,[a] for in the past you were servants of sin, but now your obedience is heart deep, and your life is being molded by truth through the teaching you are devoted to.[b] [18]And now you celebrate your freedom from your former master—sin. You've left its bondage, and now God's perfect righteousness holds power over you as his loving servants.

[19]I've used the familiar terms of a "servant" and a "master" to compensate for your weakness to understand. For just as you surrendered your bodies and souls to impurity and lawlessness, which only brought more lawlessness into your lives, so now surrender yourselves as servants of righteousness, which brings you deeper into true holiness. [20]For when you were bound as servants to sin, you lived your lives free from any obligation to righteousness.

[21]So tell me, what benefit ensued from doing those things that you're now ashamed of? It left you with nothing but a legacy of shame and death. [22]But now, as God's loving servants, you live in joyous freedom from the power of sin. So consider the benefits you now enjoy—you are brought deeper into the experience of true holiness that ends with eternal life! [23]For sin's meager wages is death,[c] but God's lavish gift is life eternal, found in your union with our Lord Jesus, the Anointed One.

---

a 6:17 As translated from the Aramaic. The Greek is "Thanks be to God."

b 6:17 As translated from the Aramaic. The Greek is "the type of teaching into which you were handed over."

c 6:23 The Greek word translated "meager wages" actually means "the wages of a foot soldier." This Greek word, *opsonion*, is taken from the word used for a piece of dried fish: *opsarion*. The Aramaic can be translated "The business of sin is death."

# Seven

## Joined to God's Anointed One

[1] I write to you, dear brothers and sisters, who are familiar with the law. Don't you know that when a person dies, it ends his obligation to the law? [2] For example, a married couple is bound by the law to remain together until separated by death. But when one spouse dies, the other is released from the law of the marriage. [3] So then if a wife is joined to another man while still married, she commits adultery. But if her husband dies, she is obviously free from the marriage contract and may marry another man without being charged with adultery.[a]

[4] So, my dear brothers and sisters, the same principle applies to your relationship with God. For you died to *your first husband*, the law, by being co-crucified with the body of the Messiah. So you are now free to "marry" another—the one who was raised from the dead so that you may now bear spiritual fruit[b] for God.

[5] When we were merely living natural lives,[c] the law, *through defining sin*, actually awakened sinful desires within us, which resulted in bearing the fruit of death. [6] But now that we have been fully released from the power of the law, we are dead to what once controlled us. And our lives are no longer motivated by the obsolete way of following the written code,[d] so that now we may serve God by living in the freshness of a new life in the power of the Holy Spirit.[e]

---

a 7:3 Or "If joined to another man, she is not an adulteress."
b 7:4 Or "offspring."
c 7:5 That is, before we came to know Jesus Christ.
d 7:6 Or "the oldness of the letter."
e 7:6 Or "by a new, Holy Spirit–empowered life."

## The Purpose of the Law

[7]So, what shall we say about all this? Am I suggesting that the law is sinful? Of course not! In fact, it was the law that gave us the clear definition of sin. For example, when the law said, "Do not covet,"[a] it became the catalyst to see how wrong it was for me to crave what belongs to someone else. [8]It was through God's commandment that sin was awakened in me and built its base of operation[b] within me to stir up every kind of wrong desire. For in the absence of the law, sin hides dormant.[c]

[9-10]I once lived without a clear understanding of the law, but when I heard God's commandments, sin sprang to life and brought with it a death sentence. The commandment that was intended to bring life brought me death instead. [11]Sin, by means of the commandment, built a base of operation within me, to overpower me[d] and put me to death. [12]So then, we have to conclude that the problem is not with the law itself, for the law is holy and its commandments are correct and for our good.

## Life Under the Law

[13]So, did something meant to be good become death to me? Certainly not! It was not the law but sin unmasked that produced my spiritual death. The sacred commandment merely uncovered the evil of sin so it could be seen for what it is. [14]For we know that the law is divinely

---

a 7:7 See Exodus 20:17 and Deuteronomy 5:21.
b 7:8 Or "a starting point."
c 7:8 Or "is lifeless."
d 7:11 Or "deceive me" or "lead me astray."

inspired and comes from the spiritual realm,[a] but I am a human being made of flesh and trafficked as a slave under sin's authority.[b]

[15]I'm a mystery to myself,[c] for I want to do what is right, but end up doing what my moral instincts condemn. [16]And if my behavior is not in line with my desire, my conscience still confirms the excellence of the law. [17]And now I realize that it is no longer my true self doing it, but the unwelcome intruder of sin in my humanity. [18]For I know that nothing good lives within the flesh of my fallen humanity. The longings to do what is right are within me, but willpower is not enough to accomplish it.[d] [19]My lofty desires to do what is good are dashed when I do the things I want to avoid. [20]So if my behavior contradicts my desires to do good, I must conclude that it's not my true identity doing it, but the unwelcome intruder of sin *hindering me from being who I really am.*

[21]Through my experience of this principle, I discover that even when I want to do good, evil is ready to sabotage me. [22]Truly, deep within my true identity, I love to do what pleases God. [23]But I discern another power operating in my humanity, waging a war against the moral principles of my conscience[e] and bringing me into captivity as a prisoner to the "law" of sin—this unwelcome intruder in my humanity. [24]What an

---

a 7:14 Or "is spiritual (comes from the spiritual realm)."

b 7:14 Or "sold and ruined under sin." The Greek word *piprasko* refers to a slave who is "sold for exportation, betrayed and ruined."

c 7:15 Paul's use of "I" is most likely his identification with the people of Israel under the law prior to receiving Christ. It is not merely an autobiographical statement that Paul experienced all of these things, but a rhetorical device of solidarity with the experience of those who live under the law. Romans chapter seven is not the present experience of any one person, but the testimony of a delivered person describing the condition of an undelivered one.

d 7:18 Some Greek manuscripts have "but I don't know how to do it."

e 7:23 As translated from the Aramaic. The Greek is "warring against the law of my mind."

agonizing situation I am in! So who has the power to rescue this miserable man from the unwelcome intruder of sin and death?[a] [25]I give all my thanks to God, for his mighty power has finally provided a way out through our Lord Jesus, the Anointed One! So if left to myself, the flesh is aligned with the law of sin, but now my renewed mind is fixed on and submitted to God's righteous principles.[b]

---

a 7:24 Or "Who will free me from this body of death?"
b 7:25 Or "God's law."

## Living by the Power of the Holy Spirit

¹*So now the case is closed.* There remains no accusing voice of condemnation against those who are joined in life-union with Jesus, the Anointed One.[a] ²For the "law" of the Spirit of life flowing through the anointing of Jesus has liberated us[b] from the "law" of sin and death. ³For God achieved what the law was unable to accomplish, because the law was limited by the weakness of human nature.[c]

Yet God sent us his Son in human form to identify with human weakness. Clothed with humanity, God's Son gave his body to be the sin-offering so that God could once and for all condemn the guilt and power of sin. ⁴So now every righteous requirement of the law can be fulfilled through the Anointed One living his life in us. And we are free to live, not according to our flesh, but by the dynamic power of the Holy Spirit![d]

⁵Those who are motivated by the flesh only pursue what benefits themselves. But those who live by the impulses of the Holy Spirit are

---

a 8:1 Or "Those who are in Christ Jesus cannot be condemned." Although there are some manuscripts that add to this verse "for those who do not walk according to the flesh but according to the Spirit," the addition is not supported by the oldest and most reliable Greek manuscripts.

b 8:2 Some Greek manuscripts have "sets me free" or "sets you (singular) free."

c 8:3 Or "weakness of the flesh."

d 8:4 What joyous truths are found in Romans 8! All that God requires of us has been satisfied by the sacrifice of Jesus Christ. The life of Jesus in us is enough to satisfy God. The power of our new life is not the works of our weak humanity, but the dynamic power of the Holy Spirit released in us.

motivated to pursue spiritual realities.[a] [6]For the mind-set of the flesh is death, but the mind-set controlled by the Spirit finds life and peace.

[7]In fact, the mind-set focused on the flesh fights God's plan and refuses to submit to his direction,[b] because it cannot! [8]For no matter how hard they try, God finds no pleasure with those who are controlled by the flesh. [9]But when the Spirit of Christ empowers your life,[c] you are not dominated by the flesh but by the Spirit. And if you are not joined to the Spirit of the Anointed One, you are not of him.[d]

[10]Now Christ lives his life in you! And even though your body may be dead because of the effects of sin, his life-giving Spirit imparts life to you because you are fully accepted by God.[e] [11]Yes, God raised Jesus to life! And since God's Spirit of Resurrection lives in you, he will also raise your dying body to life by the same Spirit that breathes life into you!

[12]So then, beloved ones, the flesh has no claims on us at all, and we have no further obligation to live in obedience to it. [13]For when you live controlled by the flesh, you are about to die. But if the life of the Spirit puts to death the corrupt ways of the flesh, we then taste his abundant life.

---

a 8:5 Or "the things of the (Holy) Spirit"; that is, doing what pleases God. This verse in the Aramaic reads, "Those who are in the flesh see him only in the flesh, but those who are in the Spirit see him in the Spirit."

b 8:7 Or "refuses to submit to his law."

c 8:9 Or "makes his home in you."

d 8:9 This is an unusual Greek clause that can be translated "If anyone is not joined to the Spirit of Christ, he cannot be himself." A similar construction is used in Luke 15:17: "The prodigal son came to himself."

e 8:10 The Aramaic is "for the cause of righteousness."

## Sons and Daughters Destined for Glory

[14]The mature children of God are those[a] who are moved by the impulses of the Holy Spirit. [15]And you did not receive the "spirit of religious duty,"[b] leading you back into the fear *of never being good enough.*[c] But you have received the "Spirit of Full Acceptance,"[d] enfolding you into the family of God. And you will never feel orphaned, for as he rises up within us, our spirits join him in saying the words of tender affection, "Beloved Father!"[e] [16]For the Holy Spirit makes God's fatherhood real to us as he whispers into our innermost being, "You are God's beloved child!"

[17]And since we are his true children, we qualify to share all his treasures, for indeed, we are heirs of God himself. And since we are joined to Christ, we also inherit all that he is and all that he has.[f] We will experi-

---

a 8:14 The Greek is quite emphatic: "those and only those."

b 8:15 Or "spirit of slavery."

c 8:15 Implied in both the text and the greater context of finding our true life in the *Spirit of Acceptance.* It can also refer to the *fear* of judgment that has been removed from us through Christ.

d 8:15 Or "spirit of adult (complete) sonship." The Aramaic is "the spirit of consecrated children."

e 8:15 *Abba* is not a Greek word, but an Aramaic word transliterated into Greek letters. Abba is the Aramaic word for "father." It is also found in Mark 14:36 and Galatians 4:6. Abba is also a word used for devotion, a term of endearment. This is why some have concluded that Abba could be translated as "Daddy" or "Papa." It is hard to imagine a closer relationship to have with God than to call him "Abba, our Beloved Father."

f 8:17 Or "We are joint-heirs with Christ." Nothing in the Bible could be more amazing than this. Grace has made former rebels into princes and princesses, royal ones that share in the inheritance of Christ.

ence being co-glorified with him provided that we accept his sufferings[a] as our own.[b]

## A Glorious Destiny

[18]I am convinced that any suffering we endure is less than nothing compared to the magnitude of glory[c] that is about to be unveiled within us.[d] [19]The entire universe is standing on tiptoe,[e] yearning to see the unveiling of God's glorious[f] sons and daughters! [20]For against its will the universe itself has had to endure the empty futility[g] resulting from the consequences of human sin. But now, with eager expectation, [21]all creation longs for freedom from its slavery to decay and to experience with us

---

[a] 8:17 Or "accept his feelings (of pain), things (he experiences)." By implication, "sufferings."

[b] 8:17 Or "If we suffer jointly we will enjoy glory jointly."

[c] 8:18 The Greek word *doxa* can also be translated "radiant beauty, splendor, perfection."

[d] 8:18 The Aramaic is "with the glory which is to be perfected in us." The Greek participle *eis* can be translated "into us," "upon us," or "to us."

[e] 8:19 The Greek word used here means "intense anticipation," or "anxiously anticipating what is about to happen (with an outstretched neck)."

[f] 8:19 Or "the manifestation of the sons of God." Interestingly, the Greek word used for "unveiling" (*apokalupsis*) is the same word for the title of the last book of the Bible, "The Revelation (Unveiling) of Jesus Christ." The created universe is but the backdrop for the dramatic appearing of God's sons and daughters unveiled with the glory of Jesus Christ upon them. The verb tense in the Greek text is clear that this "unveiling" is imminent, soon to happen, and destined to take place. Christ's glory will come to us, enter us, fill us, envelop us, and then be revealed through us as partakers of the glory. Although God will not share his glory with any other, we are no longer "another," for we are one with the Father, Son, and Holy Spirit through faith in Christ. See John 17:21–23.

[g] 8:20 Or "the purposelessness" or "the frustration (chaos)."

the wonderful freedom coming to God's children when they are glorified.[a] [22]To this day we are aware of the universal agony and groaning of creation, as if it were in the contractions of labor for childbirth. [23]And it's not just creation. We who have already experienced the first fruits of the Spirit[b] also inwardly groan as we passionately long to experience our full status as God's sons and daughters—including our physical bodies being transformed. [24]For this is the hope of our salvation.

But hope means that we must trust and wait for what is still unseen. For why would we need to hope for something we already have? [25]So because our hope is set on what is yet to be seen, we patiently keep on waiting for its fulfillment.

[26]And in a similar way, the Holy Spirit takes hold of us in our human frailty to empower us in our weakness. For example, at times we don't even know how to pray, or know the best things to ask for. But the Holy Spirit rises up within us to super-intercede[c] on our behalf, pleading to God with emotional sighs[d] too deep for words.

---

[a] 8:21 Implied in the text and the context of Romans 8:18–30.

[b] 8:23 The first fruits of the Spirit would include his indwelling presence, his gifts, his wisdom, and his transforming power. Imagine what the full harvest of the Spirit will bring to us! The Aramaic can be translated "the awakening of the Spirit."

[c] 8:26 The Greek word *hupererentugkhano* is best translated "super (or hyper)-intercede for us." We can only imagine how many blessings have poured into our lives because of the hyper-intercession of the Holy Spirit for us!

[d] 8:26 Or "groanings." We find three groanings in this chapter. Creation groans for the glorious freedom of God's children, we groan to experience the fullness of our status as God's children, and the Holy Spirit groans for our complete destiny to be fulfilled.

27God, the searcher of the heart, knows fully our longings,[a] yet he also understands the desires of the Spirit, because the Holy Spirit passionately pleads before God for us, his holy ones, in perfect harmony with God's plan and our destiny.

28So we are convinced that every detail of our lives is continually woven together to fit into God's perfect plan of bringing good into our lives, for we are his lovers who have been called to fulfill his designed purpose. 29For he knew all about us before we were born and he destined us[b] from the beginning to share the likeness of his Son. This means the Son is the oldest among a vast family of brothers and sisters who will become just like him.[c]

30 Having determined our destiny ahead of time, he called us to himself and transferred his perfect righteousness to everyone he called. And those who possess his perfect righteousness he co-glorified with his Son!

## The Triumph of God's Love

31So, what does all this mean? If God has determined to stand with us, tell me, who then could ever stand against us? 32For God has proved his love by giving us his greatest treasure, the gift of his Son. And since God freely offered him up as the sacrifice for us all,[d] he certainly won't withhold from us anything else he has to give.

---

a 8:27 Or "God, the heart-searcher." God searches our hearts not just to uncover what is wrong, but to fulfill the true desire of our hearts to be fully his. Grace triumphs over judgment.

b 8:29 The Aramaic is "sealed us (with God's mark upon us)." See also Colossians 3:4 and Hebrews 2:11.

c 8:29 Or "the eldest among a vast family of brothers and sisters."

d 8:32 This is an intentional echo of Genesis 22:16. Although God spared Abraham's son, Isaac, he would not spare his own Son, Jesus Christ.

33Who then would dare to accuse those whom God has chosen in love to be his? God himself is the judge who has issued his final verdict over them—"Not guilty!"[a]

34Who then is left to condemn us? Certainly not Jesus, the Anointed One! For he gave his life for us, and even more than that, he has conquered death and is now risen, exalted, and enthroned by God at his right hand. So how could he possibly condemn us since he is continually praying *for our triumph?*[b]

35Who could ever separate us from the endless love of God's Anointed One? *Absolutely no one!* For nothing in the universe has the power to diminish his love toward us. Troubles, pressures, and problems are unable to come between us and heaven's love. What about persecutions, deprivations,[c] dangers, and death threats? No, for they are all impotent to hinder omnipotent love, 36even though it is written:

> **All day long we face death threats for your sake, God.**
> **We are considered to be nothing more**
> **than sheep to be slaughtered![d]**

---

a 8:33 See Isaiah 50:8.

b 8:34 Implied in the text. Not only does the Holy Spirit pray for us, so does Jesus Christ. Two divine intercessors are praying for you each day. Two-thirds of the Trinity are actively engaged in intercession for us. This is typified by the incident of Moses interceding on the mountain for Israel's victory with one hand held high by Aaron (the high priest, a type of Jesus, our High Priest) and Hur (or "light," a metaphor for the Holy Spirit, who prays with divine illumination for our good). See Exodus 17:9–13, Hebrews 7:25, and Hebrews 9:24.

c 8:35 Or "hunger and nakedness."

d 8:36 See Psalm 44:22.

³⁷Yet even in the midst of all these things, we triumph over them all, for God has made us to be more than conquerors,ᵃ and his demonstrated love is our glorious victory over everything!ᵇ

³⁸So now I live with the confidence that there is nothing in the universe with the power to separate us from God's love. I'm convinced that his love will triumph over death, life's troubles,ᶜ fallen angels, or dark rulers in the heavens. There is nothing in our present or future circumstances that can weaken his love. ³⁹There is no power above us or beneath us—no power that could ever be found in the universe that can distance us from God's passionate love, which is lavished upon us through our Lord Jesus, the Anointed One!

---

ₐ 8:37 Love has made us more than conquerors in four ways: 1) No situation in life can defeat us or dilute God's love. 2) We know that divine love and power work for us to triumph over all things. 3) We share in the victory spoils of every enemy we face (Isaiah 53:12). And 4) We have conquered the Conqueror with merely a glance of our worshipping eyes. We have won his heart (Song of Songs 4:9 and 6:5).

ᵦ 8:37 Clearly implied in the text with the Greek word *hupernikao*. The love of God gives us "a glorious hyper-victory," more than can be described or contained in one word. God's love and grace has made us hyper-conquerors, empowered to be unrivaled, more than a match for any foe!

ᵧ 8:38 Or "life"; by implication, the troubles and pressures life may bring.

# *Nine*

## Paul's Love for the Jewish People

1-2O Israel, my Jewish family,[a] I feel such great sorrow and heartache for you that never leaves me! God knows these deep feelings within me as I long for you to come to faith in the Anointed One. My conscience will not let me speak anything but the truth. 3-4For my grief is so intense that I wish that I would be accursed, cut off from the Messiah, if it would mean that you, my people, would come to faith in him!

You are Israelites, my fellow citizens, and God's chosen people.[b] To you belong God's glorious presence, the covenants, the Torah, the temple with its required sacrifices, and the promises of God. 5We trace our beginnings back to the patriarchs, and through their bloodline is the genealogy of the Messiah, who is God over everything. May he be praised through endless ages! Amen!

6Clearly, God has not failed to fulfill his promises to Israel, for that will never happen! But not everyone who has descended from Israel belongs to Israel. 7Physical descent from Abraham doesn't guarantee the inheritance, because God has said:

> **"Through Isaac your descendants will be counted as part of your lineage."**[c]

8This confirms that it is not merely the natural offspring of Abraham who are considered the children of God; rather, the children born

---

a 9:1–2 Although implied here, Paul indeed calls them "my people" in verse 3.

b 9:3–4 Or "to you belong the adoption as sons."

c 9:7 Implied in the text both here and in Genesis 21:12.

because of God's promise[a] are counted as descendants. [9]For God promised Abraham:

**"In nine months from now your wife, Sarah, will have a son!"[b]**

## God's Freedom of Choice

[10]Now, this son was our ancestor, Isaac, who, with his wife, Rebekah, conceived twins. [11-12]And before her twin sons were born, God spoke to Rebekah and said:

**"The oldest will serve the younger."[c]**

God spoke these words before the sons had done anything good or bad, which proves that God calls people not on the basis of their good or bad works, but according to his divine purpose. [13]For in the words of Scripture:

**"Jacob I have chosen, but Esau I have rejected."[d]**

[14]So, what does all this mean? Are we saying that God is unfair? Of course not! [15]He had every right to say to Moses:

---

a 9:8 The Aramaic is "the children of the kingdom." By implication, it is those who can be traced back to a supernatural birth who are regarded as the children of God.

b 9:9 See Genesis 18:10, 14.

c 9:11–12 See Genesis 25:23.

d 9:13 Or "Jacob I loved, Esau I hated." The love/hate contrast is not merely a matter of God's emotions, but God's actions of choosing Jacob and excluding Esau. This Semitic idiom is also found in Jesus' words of "hating our father, mother...even our own life." It is a "hatred" compared to the love we demonstrate by choosing to follow Jesus. See Malachi 1:2–3 and Luke 14:26.

**"I will be merciful to whoever I choose and I will show compassion to whomever I wish."**[a]

[16]Again, this proves that God's choice doesn't depend on how badly someone wants it or tries to earn it,[b] but it depends on God's kindness and mercy. [17]For just as God said to Pharaoh:

**"I raised you up**[c] **as ruler of Egypt for this reason, that I might make you an example of how I demonstrate my miracle power. For by the example of how I deal with you, my powerful name will be a message proclaimed throughout the earth!"**[d]

[18]So again we see that it is entirely up to God to show mercy or to harden[e] the hearts of whomever he chooses.

[19]Well then, one might ask, "If God is in complete control, how could he blame us? For who can resist whatever he wants done?"

[20]But who do you think you are to second-guess God? How could a human being molded out of clay say to the one who molded him, "Why in the world did you make me this way?"[f] [21]Or are you denying the right of the potter to make out of clay whatever he wants? Doesn't the potter have the right to make from the same lump of clay an elegant vase or an ordinary pot?

---

a 9:15 See Exodus 33:19.

b 9:16 Or "not of the one willing nor of the one running."

c 9:17 The Aramaic is "For this reason I ruined you."

d 9:17 See Exodus 9:16.

e 9:18 Although the Greek implies God hardens hearts, the Aramaic is more of a Hebrew idiom, "God gives permission for them to be hardened." This implies the hardening the heart is from within the individual.

f 9:20 By implication Paul is speaking of people who have been made from clay in the hands of the divine Potter. See Isaiah 29:16 and 45:9.

²²And in the same way, although God has every right to unleash his anger and demonstrate his power, yet he is extremely patient with those who deserve wrath—vessels prepared for destruction. ²³And doesn't he also have the right[a] to release the revelation of the wealth of his glory to his vessels of mercy, whom God prepared beforehand to receive his glory? ²⁴Even for us, whether we are Jews or non-Jews, we are those he has called to experience his glory. ²⁵Remember the prophecy God gave in Hosea:

**"To those who were rejected and not my people,**
**    I will say to them: 'You are mine.'**
**And to those who were unloved I will say:**
**    'You are my darling.'"[b]**

²⁶And:

**"In the place where they were told, 'You are nobody,'**
**    this will be the very place where they will be renamed**
**    'Children of the Living God.'"[c]**

²⁷And the prophet Isaiah cries out to Israel:

**Though the children of Israel**
**    are as many as the sands of the seashore,**
**    only a remnant will be saved,**
**²⁸For the Lord Yahweh[d] will act**
**    and carry out his word on the earth,**

---

a 9:23 Or "This he did to make known." Although this sentence presents an anacoluthon and is missing the conditional clause, it is more likely that Paul is contrasting "the vessels prepared for destruction" with "the vessels of mercy." Thus, "And doesn't he also have the right?"

b 9:25 See Hosea 2:23.

c 9:26 See Hosea 1:10.

d 9:28 As translated from the Aramaic, "Lord YHWH."

**and waste no time to accomplish it!**[a]

[29] Just as Isaiah saw it coming and prophesied:

> **If the Lord God of angel armies**[b]
> **had not left us a remnant,**[c]
> **we would have been destroyed like Sodom**
> **and left desolate like Gomorrah!**

## Israel's Unbelief

[30] So then, what does all this mean? Here's the irony:[d] The non-Jewish people, who weren't even pursuing righteousness, were the ones who seized it—a perfect righteousness that is transferred by faith. [31] Yet Israel, even though pursuing a legal righteousness,[e] did not attain to it. [32] And why was that? Because they did not pursue the path of faith but insisted on pursuing righteousness by works,[f] as if it could be seized another way. *They were offended by the means of obtaining it*[g] and stumbled over the Stumbling Stone, [33] just as it is written:

> **"Be careful! I am setting in Zion a stone**
> **that will cause people to stumble,**

---

a 9:28 Or "cutting it short," a Greek word found only here in the New Testament. See Isaiah 10:23.

b 9:29 As translated from the Aramaic, "Lord YHWH of hosts (of angel armies)."

c 9:29 Or "descendants." See Isaiah 1:9.

d 9:30 Implied in the text.

e 9:31 Or "a righteousness based on the law."

f 9:32 Or "works of the law."

g 9:32 Implied and made explicit to define the metaphor of stumbling over the Stumbling Stone.

a rock[a] of offence that will make them fall,
but believers in him will not experience shame."[b]

---

[a] 9:33 There is a play on words here that is lost in translation. The Aramaic word for "rock" (*keefa*) is also the word for "teaching" or "faith." Aramaic speakers today still say that to stand in faith means to stand on a rock. To speak of the message of faith for salvation (versus works) is hidden in the word *rock*.

[b] 9:33 See Isaiah 8:14 and 28:16. The Hebrew of Isaiah 28:16 is "Let the one who believes not expect it soon." That is, even if a promise delays, we will not be disheartened but will remain steadfast in faith.

## Ten

### Faith-Righteousness

[1]My beloved brothers and sisters, the passionate desire of my heart and constant prayer to God is for my fellow Israelites to experience salvation. [2]For I know that although they are deeply devoted to God, they are unenlightened. [3]And since they've ignored the righteousness God gives, wanting instead to be acceptable to God because of their own works, they've refused to submit to God's faith-righteousness. [4]For the Christ is the end of the law.[a] And because of him, God has transferred his perfect righteousness to all who believe.

[5]Moses wrote long ago about the need to obey every part of the law in order to be declared right with God:

> **"The one who obeys these things must always live by them."**[b]

[6]But we receive the faith-righteousness that speaks an entirely different message:

> **"Don't for a moment think you need to climb into the heavens to find the Messiah and bring him down,**

> [7]**or to descend into the underworld to bring him up from the dead."**[c]

[8]But the faith-righteousness we receive speaks to us in these words of Moses:

---

[a] 10:4 Or "Christ is the goal of the law."
[b] 10:5 Or "Whoever obeys these things will find life." See Leviticus 18:5.
[c] 10:7 See Deuteronomy 30:12–13.

> "God's living message is very close to you, as close as
> your own heart beating in your chest and as near as the
> tongue in your mouth."[a]

[9]And what is God's "living message"? It is the revelation of faith for salvation,[b] which is the message that we preach. For if you publicly declare with your mouth that Jesus is Lord and believe in your heart that God raised him from the dead, you will experience salvation. [10]The heart that believes in him receives the gift of the righteousness of God—and then the mouth gives thanks[c] to salvation. [11]For the Scriptures encourage us with these words:

> "Everyone who believes in him will never be
> disappointed."[d]

## Good News for All People

[12]So then faith eliminates the distinction between Jew and non-Jew, for he is the same Lord Jehovah[e] for all people. And he has enough treasures to lavish generously upon all who call on him. [13]And it's true:

> "Everyone who calls on the name of the Lord Yahweh
> will be rescued and experience new life."[f]

[14]But how can people call on him for help if they've not yet believed? And how can they believe in one they've not yet heard of? And how can they hear the message of life if there is no one there to proclaim it?

---

a 10:8 See Deuteronomy 30:14.

b 10:9 Or "word of faith."

c 10:10 As translated from the Aramaic. The Greek is "the mouth confesses to salvation."

d 10:11 See Isaiah 28:16.

e 10:12 As translated from the Aramaic.

f 10:13 As translated from the Aramaic. See Joel 2:32.

15And how can the message be proclaimed if messengers have yet to be sent? That's why the Scriptures say:

> **How welcome is the arrival**[a]
> **of those proclaiming the joyful news of peace**
> **and of good things to come!**

16But not everyone welcomes[b] the good news, as Isaiah said:

> **Lord, is there anyone who hears**
> **and believes our message?**[c]

17Faith, then, is birthed in a heart that responds to God's anointed utterance of the Anointed One.[d]

18Can it be that Israel hasn't heard the message? No, they have heard it, for:

> **The voice has been heard throughout the world,**
> **and its message has gone to the ends of the earth!**[e]

19So again I ask, didn't Israel already understand that God's message was for others as well as for themselves?[f] *Yes, they certainly did understand,*[g] for Moses was the first[h] to state it:

---

a 10:15 Or "how beautiful the feet." The Greek word implies their arrival comes at just the right time. See Isaiah 52:7 and Nahum 1:15.

b 10:16 Or "obeys."

c 10:16 See Isaiah 53:1.

d 10:17 Or "the utterance of the Anointed One." The Greek word *rhema* carries a focus on the preached (spoken) word. The Aramaic is "Faith is from the hearing ear, and the hearing ear is from the Word of God."

e 10:18 See Psalm 19:4.

f 10:19 Implied in the context. Paul is confirming that God's plan from the beginning was to give the message of salvation to all the nations.

g 10:19 Implied as the answer of the rhetorical question.

h 10:19 Or "First Moses...then Isaiah (v. 20) confirms it."

> "I will make you jealous of a people who are 'nobodies.'
> And I will use people with no understanding
> to provoke you to anger."[a]

20And Isaiah the fearless prophet dared to declare:

> "Those who found me weren't even seeking me.
> I manifested[b] myself before those
> who weren't even asking to know me!"[c]

21Yet regarding Israel Isaiah says:

> "With love I have held out my hands day after day,
> offering myself to this unbelieving
> and stubborn people!"[d]

---

a  10:19 See Deuteronomy 32:21. Those who are "not a nation" and the "sense-less nation" both refer to the Gentile believers among the nations that have by faith entered into new life in Jesus.

b  10:20 The compound Greek word *emphanes* means "to make manifest, to appear in shining light, to be bright, to shine light upon, to come into view."

c  10:20 See Isaiah 65:1.

d  10:21 See Isaiah 65:2.

# *Eleven*

## God Will Not Forget His Promises to Israel

[1]So then I ask you this question: did God really push aside and reject his people?[a] Absolutely not! For I myself am a Jew, a descendant of Abraham, from the tribe of Benjamin.[b] [2]God has not rejected his chosen, destined people![c] Haven't you heard Elijah's testimony in the Scriptures, and how he prays to God, agonizing over Israel?

> [3]**"Lord, they've murdered your prophets; they've demolished your altars. Now I'm the only one left and they want to kill me!"[d]**

[4]But what was the revelation[e] God spoke to him in response?

> **"You are not alone.[f] For I have preserved a remnant for myself—seven thousand others who are faithful and have refused to worship Baal."[g]**

---

a 11:1 See 1 Samuel 12:22 and Psalm 94:14.

b 11:1 Benjamin was the only son of Jacob born in the Promised Land, and his was the first tribe to give Israel a king in Saul. And his was the only tribe to remain with Judah in the restored nation after the exile. Paul is saying that he is about as Jewish as anyone could ever be. See Philippians 3:5.

c 11:2 Or "His people whom he foreknew."

d 11:3 See 1 Kings 19:10–14.

e 11:4 Or "divine utterance." This is the only place in the New Testament this Greek word appears. It could imply the audible voice of God that spoke to Elijah.

f 11:4 A summary statement implied in the text and made explicit for the sake of clarity.

g 11:4 See 1 Kings 19:18.

⁵And that is but one example of what God is doing in this age of fulfillment, for God's grace empowers his chosen remnant. ⁶And since it is by God's grace, it can't be a matter of their good works; otherwise, it wouldn't be a gift of grace, but earned by human effort.

⁷So then, Israel failed to achieve what it had strived for, but the divinely chosen remnant receives it by grace, while the rest were hardened *and unable to receive the truth.* ⁸Just as it is written:

> **God granted them a spirit of deep slumber.**[a]
>    **He closed their eyes to the truth**
>    **and prevented their ears from hearing**[b]
>    **up to this very day.**

⁹And King David also prophesied this:

> **May their table**[c] **prove to be a snare**
>    **and a trap to cause their ruin.**
>    **Bring them the retribution they deserve.**
>
> ¹⁰**Blindfold their eyes and don't let them see.**
>    **Let them be stooped over continually.**[d]

## The Restoration of Israel

¹¹So, am I saying that Israel stumbled so badly that they will never get back up? Certainly not! Rather, it was because of their stumble that

---

a  11:8 The Aramaic is "a spirit of frustration."

b  11:8 Or "He gave them eyes that could not see and ears that could not hear." See Deuteronomy 29:4, Isaiah 6:10, and Isaiah 29:10–13.

c  11:9 This could also be a metaphor for their false security, being in a place of well-being and favor. King David's son Absalom held a banquet as a pretense to murder his brother Amnon. See 2 Samuel 13:23–31.

d  11:10 This could also be a metaphor of asking God to punish them. See LXX of Psalm 69:22–23.

salvation now extends to all the non-Jewish people, in order to make Israel jealous and desire the very things that God has freely given them. [12]So if all the world is being greatly enriched through their failure, and through their fall great spiritual wealth is given to the non-Jewish people, imagine how much more will Israel's awakening[a] bring to us all!

[13]Now, I speak to you who are not Jewish, since I am an apostle to reach the non-Jewish people. And I draw attention to this ministry as much as I can when I am among the Jews, [14]hoping to make them jealous of what God has given to those who are not Jews, winning some of my people to salvation.

[15]For if their *temporary*[b] rejection released the reconciling power of grace into the world, what will happen when Israel is reinstated and reconciled to God? It will unleash resurrection power throughout the whole earth!

## A Warning to Non-Jewish Believers

[16]Since Abraham and the patriarchs are consecrated and set apart for God, so also will their descendants be set apart.[c] If the roots of a tree are holy and set apart for God, so too will be the branches.

---

a 11:12 Or "fullness (of restoration)" or "full inclusion" or "full number." An ellipsis in the Greek text allows for different translations of this verse.

b 11:15 Implied in the context.

c 11:16 Paul uses a metaphor that is better understood when made explicit. The Greek is literally "If the first portion of the dough (Abraham and the patriarchs) is consecrated, so too is the entire batch of dough (those descended from Abraham and the patriarchs)." The principle is that if the first portion is dedicated to God, the rest belongs to him too and is also considered consecrated for God's use. The Aramaic is "If the crust is holy, so also is the dough."

¹⁷However, some of the branches have been pruned away. And you,ᵃ who were once nothing more than a wild olive branch in the desert,ᵇ God has grafted in—inserting you among the remaining branches as a joint partner to share in the wonderful richness of the cultivated olive stem. ¹⁸So don't be so arrogant as to believe that you are superior to the natural branches. There's no reason to boast, for the new branches don't support the root, but you owe your life to the root that supports you!

¹⁹You might begin to think that some branches were pruned or broken off just to make room for you. ²⁰Yes, that's true.ᶜ They were removed because of their unbelief. But remember this: you are only attached by your faith. So don't be presumptuous, but stand in awe and reverence. ²¹Since God didn't spare the natural branches that fell into unbelief, perhaps he won't spare you either!

²²So fix your gaze on the simultaneous kindnessᵈ and strict justiceᵉ of God. How severely he treated those who fell into unbelief! Yet how tender and kind is his relationship with you. So keep on trusting in his kindness; otherwise, you also will be cut off.

---

ᵃ 11:17 Every time "you" is used in verses 17–24 it is singular. God has lovingly and personally grafted you in as a branch in his tree of life. See John 15:1–17.

ᵇ 11:17 As translated from the Aramaic.

ᶜ 11:20 The Aramaic is "Yes, it's beautiful!" Non-Jewish believers are to be grateful for the Jewish roots of our faith. Our Messiah is Jewish and the Scriptures we read were given to the beloved Jewish people. We feast on the new-covenant riches that have been handed down to us through the "olive tree" of Judaism.

ᵈ 11:22 The Aramaic word for kindness is also translated "sweetness."

ᵉ 11:22 The Greek word apotomia is used only here in the New Testament. It is a play on words, for apotomia is a homonym that can mean "strict justice" or "cut off."

²³God is more than ready to graft back in the natural branches when they turn from clinging to their unbelief to embracing faith. ²⁴For if God grafted you in, even though you were taken from what is by nature a wild olive tree, how much more can he reconnect the natural branches by inserting them back into their own cultivated olive tree!

## The Mystery of Israel's Restoration

²⁵My beloved brothers and sisters, I want to share with you[a] a mystery[b] concerning Israel's future. For understanding this mystery will keep you from thinking you already know everything.

A partial and temporary hardening[c] to the gospel has come over Israel, which will last until the full number of non-Jews has come into God's family. ²⁶And then God will bring all of Israel to salvation! The prophecy will be fulfilled that says:

> **"Coming from Zion will be the Savior,**
> **and he will turn Jacob away from evil.**[d]
> ²⁷**For this is my covenant promise with them**
> **when I forgive their sins."**[e]

---

a 11:25 The Greek text contains a litotes, a double negative: "I don't want you to not know."

b 11:25 The Greek word for mystery, *mystērion*, is found twenty-eight times in the New Testament. It means a sacred secret, something that God has hidden from ancient times and that can only be revealed by God. Jesus teaches us that these mysteries are meant for us to perceive as part of our kingdom birthright. See Matthew 13:11. The mystery Paul unfolds for us here is the partial insensitivity of Israel, as well as her future salvation as part of God's eternal plan for the nations.

c 11:25 The Greek word for hardening, *porosis,* can also mean stubbornness, an unwillingness to learn something new.

d 11:26 The Aramaic can also mean "the evil one." See Isaiah 59:20–21.

e See Isaiah 27:9.

²⁸Now, many of the Jews are opposed to the gospel, but their opposition has opened the door of the gospel to you who are not Jewish. Yet they are still greatly loved by God because their ancestors were divinely chosen to be his. ²⁹And when God chooses someone and graciously imparts gifts to him, they are never rescinded.[a]

³⁰You who are not Jews were once rebels against God, but now, because of their disobedience, you have experienced God's tender mercies. ³¹And now they are the rebels, and because of God's tender mercies to you, you can open the door to them to share in and enjoy what God has given to us!

³²Actually, God considers all of humanity to be prisoners of their unbelief, so that he can unlock our hearts and show his tender mercies to all who come to him.

³³Who could ever wrap their minds around the riches of God, the depth of his wisdom, and the marvel of his perfect knowledge? Who could ever explain the wonder of his decisions[b] or search out the mysterious way he carries out his plans?

> ³⁴**For who has discovered how the Lord thinks**
> **or is wise enough to be the one**
> **to advise him in his plans?**[c]

³⁵Or:

> **"Who has ever first given something to God**
> **that obligates God to owe him something in return?"**[d]

---

a 11:29 Or "the grace-gifts and calling of God are void of regret and without change in purpose." See Isaiah 27:9 and Jeremiah 31:33–34.

b 11:33 Or "judgments," which does not necessarily imply something negative.

c 11:34 See Isaiah 40:13.

d 11:35 See Job 41:11.

<sup>36</sup>And because God is the source and sustainer of everything, everything finds fulfillment in him. May all praise and honor be given to him forever! Amen!

*Twelve*

## The Transforming Power of the Gospel

[1]Beloved friends, what should be our proper response to God's marvelous mercies? I encourage you to surrender yourselves to God to be his sacred, living sacrifices. And live in holiness, experiencing all that delights his heart. For this becomes your genuine expression of worship.

[2]Stop imitating the ideals and opinions of the culture around you,[a] but be inwardly transformed by the Holy Spirit through a total reformation of how you think. This will empower you to discern God's will as you live a beautiful life, satisfying and perfect in his eyes.

## Your Proper Role in the Body of Christ

[3]God has given me grace to speak a warning about pride. I would ask each of you to be emptied of self-promotion, and not create a false image of your importance. Instead, honestly assess your worth by using your God-given faith as the standard of measurement, and then you will see your true value with an appropriate self-esteem.

[4]In the human body there are many parts and organs, each with a unique function. [5]And so it is in the body of Christ. For though we are many, we've all been mingled into one body in Christ. This means that we are all vitally joined to one another, with each contributing to the others.

[6]God's marvelous grace imparts to each one of us varying gifts and ministries that are uniquely ours. So if God has given you the grace-gift of prophecy, you must activate your gift by using the proportion of faith you have to prophesy. [7]If your grace-gift is serving, then thrive in serving

---

[a] 12:2 Or "Don't be squeezed into the mold of this present age."

others well. If you have the grace-gift of teaching, then be actively teaching and training others. [8]If you have the grace-gift of encouragement,[a] then use it often to encourage others. If you have the grace-gift of giving to meet the needs of others, then may you prosper in your generosity without any fanfare. If you have the gift of leadership, be passionate about your leadership. And if you have the gift of showing compassion,[b] then flourish in your cheerful[c] display of compassion.

## Transformed Relationships

[9]Let the inner movement of your heart always be to love one another, and never play the role of an actor wearing a mask. Despise evil and embrace everything that is good and virtuous.

[10]Be devoted to tenderly loving your fellow believers *as members of one family.*[d] Try to outdo yourselves in respect and honor of one another.

[11]Be enthusiastic to serve the Lord, keeping your passion toward him boiling hot! Radiate with the glow of the Holy Spirit and let him fill you with excitement as you serve him.

[12]Let this hope burst forth within you, releasing a continual joy. Don't give up in a time of trouble,[e] but commune with God at all times.

[13]Take a constant interest in the needs of God's beloved people and respond by helping them. And eagerly welcome people as guests into your home.

---

[a] 12:8 Or "exhortation." This is the Greek word *parakaleo*, which means "to be alongside of someone to comfort, encourage, console, strengthen, exhort, and stir up faith."

[b] 12:8 Or "if you are a caregiver."

[c] 12:8 The Greek word *hilarotes* is used only here in the New Testament and can be translated "cheerful" or "hilarious."

[d] 12:10 Implied in the text.

[e] 12:12 The Aramaic is "Bear your afflictions bravely."

¹⁴Speak blessing, not cursing, over those who reject and persecute you.

¹⁵Celebrate with those who celebrate, and weep with those who grieve. ¹⁶Live happily together in a spirit of harmony, and be as mindful of another's worth as you are your own. Don't live with a lofty mindset, thinking you are too important to serve others, but be willing to do menial tasks and identify with those who are humble minded.ᵃ Don't be smug or even think for a moment that you know it all.

¹⁷Never hold a grudge or try to get even, but plan your life around the noblest way to benefit others. ¹⁸Do your best to live as everybody's friend.ᵇ

¹⁹Beloved, don't be obsessed with taking revenge, but leave that to God's righteous justice.ᶜ For the Scriptures say:

> **"If you don't take justice in your own hands,**
> **I will release justice for you," says the Lord.**ᵈ

²⁰And:

> **If your enemy is hungry, buy him lunch!**
> **Win him over with kindness.**ᵉ

---

a 12:16 Since the Greek text is ambiguous and can mean either "be willing to do menial tasks" or "associate with the lowly," the translation incorporates both. The Berkeley Translation renders this "Adjust yourselves to humble situations."

b 12:18 Or "to live at peace with all people."

c 12:19 Or "wrath."

d 12:19 As translated from the Aramaic. See Deuteronomy 32:35.

e 12:20 Or "If he thirsts, give him a drink."

**For your surprising generosity will awaken his conscience, and God will reward you with favor.**[a]

[21]Never let evil defeat you, but defeat evil with good.[b]

---

[a] 12:20 Or "You will heap coals of fire on his head," an obvious figure of speech. It means that by demonstrating kindness to him, his heart will be moved and his shame exposed. See Proverbs 25:21–22.

[b] 12:21 Or "Don't be conquered by the evil one, but conquer evil through union with the Good One."

# *Thirteen*

## Our Relationship to Civil Authorities

[1]Every person must submit to and support the authorities over him. For there can be no authority in the universe except by God's appointment, which means that every authority that exists has been instituted by God. [2]So to resist authority is to resist the divine order of God, which results in severe consequences. [3]For civil authorities don't intimidate those who are doing good, but those who are doing evil. So do what is right and you'll never need to fear those in authority. They will commend you for your good citizenship.

[4]Those in authority are God's servants for the good of society. But if you break the law, you have reason to be alarmed, for they are God's agents of punishment to bring criminals to justice. Why do you think they carry weapons? [5]You are compelled to obey them, not just to avoid punishment, but because you want to live with a clean conscience.

[6]This is also the reason you pay your taxes, for governmental authorities are God's officials who oversee these things. [7]So it is your duty to pay all the taxes and fees that they require and to respect those who are worthy of respect, honoring them accordingly.[a]

[8]Don't owe anything to anyone, except your outstanding debt to continually love one another,[b] for the one who learns to love has fulfilled every requirement of the law. [9]For the commandments "Do not commit

---

[a] 13:7 Jesus was often maligned for being "the friend of tax-collectors (publicans)." Nero went down in history as one of the most cruel and unjust rulers who ever lived.

[b] 13:8 There is a pronounced play on words in the Aramaic. The Aramaic word for "owe" is khob, and the word for "love" is khab.

adultery, do not murder, do not steal, do not covet,"[a] and every other commandment can be summed up in these words:

**"Love and value others the same way you love and value yourself."**[b]

[10]Love makes it impossible to harm another, so love fulfills all that the law requires.

## Living in the Light

[11]To live like this is all the more urgent, for time is running out and you know it is a strategic hour in human history. It is time for us to wake up! For our full salvation[c] is nearer now than when we first believed.

[12]Night's darkness is dissolving away as a new day of destiny dawns.[d] So we must once and for all strip away what is done in the shadows of darkness, *removing it like filthy clothes.*[e] And once and for all we clothe ourselves with the radiance of light as our weapon. [13]We must live honorably,[f] surrounded by the light of this new day, not in the darkness of drunkenness[g] and debauchery,[h] not in promiscuity and sensuality,[i] not being argumentative or jealous of others.

---

a 13:9 See Exodus 20:13–17.

b 13:9 See Leviticus 19:18, Galatians 5:6, and 1 Corinthians 13:4–6.

c 13:11 Or "perfect wholeness." There is a full salvation ready to be unveiled and unfolded in the last days. See 1 Peter 1:5.

d 13:12 See 1 John 2:8.

e 13:12 Implied in the text and supplied to show the contrast of "clothe ourselves" in the next sentence.

f 13:13 The Aramaic can be translated "We walk with the Designer."

g 13:13 This word includes intoxication by any substance.

h 13:13 Or "festive processions (often to celebrate false deities), orgies, revelries, carousings."

i 13:13 Or "outrageous behavior, loose conduct, indecencies."

[14]Instead fully immerse yourselves into[a] the Lord Jesus, the Anointed One, and don't waste even a moment's thought on your former identity to awaken its selfish desires.

---

a 13:14 Or "fully clothed with."

# *Fourteen*

—

## Unity in the Midst of Diversity

¹Offer an open hand of fellowship to welcome every true believer, even though their faith may be weak and immature. And refuse to engage in debates with them concerning nothing more than opinions.

²For example, one believer has no problem with eating all kinds of food, but another with weaker faith will eat only vegetables.ᵃ ³The one who eats freely shouldn't judge and look down on the one who eats only vegetables. And the vegetarian must not judge and look down on the one who eats everything. Remember, God has welcomed him and taken him as his partner.

⁴Who do you think you are to sit in judgment of someone else's household servant?ᵇ His own master is the one to evaluate whether he succeeds or fails. And God's servants will succeed, for God's powerᶜ supports them and enables them to stand.

⁵In the same way, one person regards a certain day as more sacred than another, and another person regards them all alike. There is nothing wrong with having different personal convictions about such matters.ᵈ ⁶For the person who observes one day as especially sacred does it to

---

ᵃ 14:2 It is possible that the one with "weaker faith" refused to eat meat because it was offered to idols or was considered unclean.

ᵇ 14:4 We are all "household servants" in the body of Christ, for we each belong to him. When believers begin to judge other believers over our opinions or preferences, we are taking the role that belongs only to Jesus.

ᶜ 14:4 Some Greek manuscripts have "the Lord."

ᵈ 14:5 Or "Each one must be fully convinced in his own mind." The Aramaic can be translated "Every human being justifies himself through his own perspective."

honor the Lord. And the same is true regarding what a person eats. The one who eats everything eats to honor the Lord, because he gives thanks to God, and the one who has a special diet does it to honor the Lord, and he also gives thanks to God.

[7]No one lives to himself and no one dies to himself. [8]While we live, we must live for our Master, and in death we must bring honor to him. So dead or alive we belong to our Master.[a] [9]For this very reason the Anointed One died and was brought back to life again, so that he would become the Lord God[b] over both the dead and the living.[c]

[10]Why would you judge your brothers or sisters because of their diet, despising them for what they eat or don't eat? For we each will have our turn to stand before God's judgment seat.[d] [11]Just as it is written:

> **"As surely as I am the Living God, I tell you:**
> **'Every knee will bow before me**
> **and every tongue will confess the truth[e]**
> **and glorify me!'"[f]**

[12]Therefore, each one must answer for himself and give a personal account of his own life before God.

---

a 14:8 The Aramaic twice uses "our Master (Lord)," while the Greek is "the Lord."

b 14:9 Or "Lord Jehovah" (Aramaic). The Greek is *kurios* ("Lord").

c 14:9 That is, he exercises lordship over all believers: those living in faith and those who die in faith.

d 14:10 The Aramaic is "We are all destined to stand before the podium of the Messiah."

e 14:11 Or "will fully agree (speak from the same source)."

f 14:11 See Isaiah 45:23, Isaiah 49:18, and Philippians 2:10–12.

## Walking in Love

¹³So stop being critical and condemning of other believers, but instead determine to never deliberately cause a brother or sister to stumble[a] and fall because of your actions.

¹⁴I know and am convinced by personal revelation from the Lord Jesus that there is nothing wrong with eating any food. But to the one who considers it be unclean, it is unacceptable. ¹⁵If your brother or sister is offended because you insist on eating what you want, it is no longer love that rules your conduct. Why would you wound someone for whom the Messiah gave his life, just so you can eat what you want? ¹⁶So don't give people the opportunity to slander what you know to be good.[b] ¹⁷For the kingdom of God is not a matter of rules about food and drink, but is in the realm of the Holy Spirit,[c] filled with righteousness,[d]

---

a 14:13 Or "set before them an obstacle or trap to make them stumble."

b 14:16 Even today in many cultures of the world, there are two things that cause division and spark debates among religious people. The observance of "special days" (fasts, feasts, Sabbaths, days of prayer, etc.) and dietary restrictions (kosher versus non-kosher). Paul addresses both of these cultural issues as examples of things that can divide us. In every culture there are religious traditions that are observed in varying degrees. As believers, our one tradition must be to love and not offend by deliberate actions that demonstrate insensitivity to others. The overarching message Paul brings in Romans 14 is that we are obligated to walk in love and not put our preferences above love's calling to honor others. These principles are to be applied in every cultural distinction in the body of Christ.

c 14:17 The kingdom of God is entered into by the Holy Spirit, and not by observing feasts and ritual meals. We must be born of the Spirit in order to enter into God's kingdom realm. To have the Holy Spirit is to have the realities of God's kingdom.

d 14:17 *Righteousness* means, both in the context and in the Hebraic mindset, kindness in our relationships. Paul is speaking of putting others first and expressing goodness in having right relationships with others as well as right living.

peace, and joy. [18]Serving the Anointed One by walking in these king-dom realities pleases[a] God and earns the respect of others.

[19]So then, make it your top priority to live a life of peace with harmony in your relationships,[b] eagerly seeking to strengthen and encourage one another. [20]Stop ruining the work of God by insisting on your own opinions about food. You can eat anything you want,[c] but it is wrong to deliberately cause someone to be offended over what you eat. [21]*Consider it an act of love[d]* to refrain from eating meat or drinking wine or doing anything else that would cause a fellow believer to be offended or tempted to be weakened in his faith.[e] [22]Keep the convictions you have about these matters between yourself and God, *and don't impose them upon others.[f]* You'll be happy when you don't judge yourself in doing what your conscience approves. [23]But the one who has misgivings feels miserable if he eats meat, because he doubts and doesn't eat in faith. For anything we do that doesn't spring from faith is, by definition, sinful.

---

a 14:18 The Aramaic is "beautiful to God."

b 14:19 See Psalm 34:15 and Hebrews 12:14.

c 14:20 Or "All (food) is (ceremonially) clean (acceptable to eat)."

d 14:21 Implied in the context of Romans 14–15, supplied to clarify the motivation to limit our liberties among believes.

e 14:21 A few manuscripts do not have the last phrase, "or to be weakened in his faith."

f 14:22 A conclusion statement implied in the context and supplied for the sake of clarity.

## Love Is the Key to Unity

[1]Now, those who are mature[a] in their faith can easily be recognized, for they don't live to please themselves but have learned to patiently embrace others in their immaturity.[b] [2]Our goal must be to empower others to do what is right and good for them, and to bring them into spiritual maturity. [3]For not even *the most powerful one of all,*[c] the Anointed One, lived to please himself. His life fulfilled the Scripture that says:

**All the insults of those who insulted you fall upon me.**[d]

Whatever was written beforehand is meant to instruct us in how to live. The Scriptures impart to us encouragement and inspiration so that we can live in hope and endure all things.

[5]Now may God, the source of great endurance and comfort, grace you with unity among yourselves, which flows from your relationship with Jesus, the Anointed One.[e] [6]Then, with a unanimous rush of passion, you will with one voice glorify God, the Father of our Lord Jesus Christ. [7]You will bring God glory when you accept and welcome one another as partners, just as the Anointed One has fully accepted you and received you as his partner.

---

a 15:1 The Aramaic is "powerful."

b 15:1 Or "not just please themselves."

c 15:3 Implied in the context and supplied for the sake of clarity of Paul's logic.

d 15:3 See Psalm 69:9.

e 15:5 The Aramaic is "that you may value one another equally in Jesus, the Messiah."

## The God of Hope for Jews and Non-Jews

⁸I am convinced that Jesus, the Messiah, was sent as a servant to the Jewish people[a] to fulfill the promises God made to our ancestors and to prove God's faithfulness. ⁹And now, because of Jesus, the non-Jewish people of the world can glorify God for his kindness to them, fulfilling the prophecy of Scripture:

> **Because of this I will proclaim you among the nations**
> **and they will hear me sing praises to your name.**[b]

¹⁰And in another place it says:

> **"You who are not Jewish,**
> **celebrate life right alongside his Jewish people."**[c]

¹¹And again:

> **Praise the Lord Yahweh,**[d] **all you who are not Jews,**
> **and let all the people of the earth**
> **raise their voices in praises to him.**[e]

¹²And Isaiah prophesied:

> **"An heir to David's throne**[f] **will emerge,**
> **and he will rise up as ruler**

a 15:8 Or "a servant of the circumcision," which is a figure of speech for the Jewish people.

b 15:9 See Psalm 18:49.

c 15:10 See Deuteronomy 32:43.

d 15:11 As translated from the Aramaic.

e 15:11 See Psalm 117:1.

f 15:12 Or "(a sprout from) the root of Jesse," which is a Hebrew idiom for King David, the son of Jesse, who was promised to have an heir to his throne who would rule over not only Israel but all the nations.

over all the non-Jewish nations,
for all their hopes will be met in him."[a]

[13]Now may God, the inspiration and fountain of hope, fill you to overflowing with uncontainable joy and perfect peace as you trust in him. And may the power of the Holy Spirit continually surround your life with his super-abundance until you radiate with hope!

## Paul's Ministry and His Plans

[14]My dear brothers and sisters, I am fully convinced of your genuine spirituality. I know that each of you is stuffed full of God's goodness, that you are richly supplied with all kinds of revelation-knowledge, and that you are empowered to effectively instruct[b] one another. [15]And because of the outpouring of God's grace on my life to be his minister and to preach Jesus, the Anointed One, to the non-Jewish people, I have written rather boldly to you on some themes, reminding you of their importance. [16]For this grace has made me a servant of the gospel of God, constantly doing the work of a priest, for I endeavor to present an acceptable offering to God; so that the non-Jewish people of the earth may be set apart and made holy by the Spirit of holiness.

[17]Now then, it is through my union with Jesus Christ, that I enjoy an enthusiasm and confidence in my ministry for God. [18-19]And I will not be presumptuous to speak of anything except what Christ has accomplished through me. For many non-Jewish people are coming into faith's obedience by the power of the Spirit of God, which is displayed through mighty signs and amazing wonders, both in word and deed. Starting from Jerusalem I went from place to place as far as the distant Roman

---

a 15:12 Or "Their hopes will be placed on him." See Isaiah 11:10.
b 15:14 Or "warn."

province of Illyricum,[a] fully preaching the wonderful message of Christ.[b] [20]It is my honor and constant passion to be a pioneer who preaches where no one has ever even heard of the Anointed One, instead of building upon someone else's foundation. [21]As the Scriptures say:

> **Those who know nothing about him will clearly see him,**
> **and those who have not heard will respond.**[c]

## Paul's Intention to Visit Rome

[22]My pursuit of this mission has prevented me many times from visiting you, [23]but there is now nothing left to keep me in these regions. So many years I have longed to come and be with you! [24]So on my way to Spain I hope to visit you as I pass through Rome. And after I have enjoyed fellowship with you for a while, I hope that you would help me financially on my journey. [25]But now I'm on my way to Jerusalem to encourage God's people and minister to them.

[26]I am pleased to inform you that the believers of Macedonia and Greece[d] have made a generous contribution for the poor among the holy believers in Jerusalem. [27]They were thrilled to have an opportunity to give back to the believers in Jerusalem. For indeed, they are deeply grateful for them and feel indebted because they brought them the

---

a 15:18-19 Illyricum (Croatia) was the Roman province that comprises parts of the western Balkan Peninsula.

b 15:18-19 The apostle Paul thoroughly preached the good news with much evidence that God was working through him. This resulted in many non-Jewish people coming to faith in Jesus Christ. The signs and wonders were a part of the message, validating Paul's apostolic mandate to evangelize and plant churches.

c 15:21 As translated from the Aramaic. The Greek is "understand." See Isaiah 52:15.

d 15:26 Or "Achaia," a region in western Greece.

gospel. Since the ethnic multitudes have shared in the spiritual wealth of the Jewish people, it is only right that the non-Jewish people share their material wealth with them.

²⁸So, when I have completed this act of worship and safely delivered the offering[a] to them in Jerusalem, I will set out for Spain and visit you on my way there. ²⁹I am convinced that when I come to you, I will come packed full and loaded[b] with the blessings of the Anointed One!

³⁰That's why I plead with you, because of our union with our Lord Jesus Christ, to be partners with me in your prayers to God. My dear brothers and sisters in the faith, with the love we share in the Holy Spirit, fight alongside me in prayer.[c] ³¹Ask the Father to deliver me from the danger I face from the unbelievers in Judea. For I want to make sure that the contribution I carry for Jerusalem will be favorably received by God's holy ones. ³²Then he will send me to you with great joy in the pleasure of God's will, and I will be spiritually refreshed by your fellowship.

³³And now may the God who gives us his peace and wholeness,[d] be with you all. Yes, Lord, so let it be!

---

a 15:28 The Greek word is actually "fruit." Paul was delivering to them a "spiritual fruit basket." It is an act of worship every time we consider the poor and serve others.

b 15:29 The Greek word *pleroma* is also used for a cargo ship packed full of people and goods.

c 15:30 Although Paul was an esteemed and powerful apostle of Jesus, he was not too proud to ask other believers to pray for him.

d 15:33 Or "May the God who is peace be with you all."

# *Sixteen*

## Paul Sends His Loving Greetings

[1]Now, let me introduce to you our dear and beloved sister in the faith, Phoebe, a shining servant[a] of the church in Cenchrea.[b] [2]I am sending her with this letter and ask that you shower her with your hospitality when she arrives. Embrace her with honor, as is fitting for one who belongs to the Lord and is set apart for him. I am entrusting her to you,[c] so provide her whatever she may need, for she's been a great leader and champion[d] for many—I know, for she's been that for even me!

---

[a] 16:1 Or "deaconess" or "minister," which would imply she may have held an office in the church. The name Phoebe means "shining, radiant, bright, prophetic." It is likely that the church in Cenchrea was a house church.

[b] 16:1 Or modern-day Kenchreai, which in the days of Paul was a large port city seven kilometers southeast of Corinth in Greece. See also Acts 18:18.

[c] 16:2 As translated from the Aramaic and implied in the Greek.

[d] 16:2 The Greek word *prostatis* means "the one who goes first, a leading officer presiding over many, a protecting patroness who oversees the affairs of others, a champion defender." It is clear that Phoebe was considered a leader, a champion, a heroic woman who was most likely quite wealthy and brought blessings to others. The term *prostatis* implies a great status (as used in classical Greek) and denotes a high position in the church. Paul honors a total of thirty-seven people in this last chapter of Romans. Their names have gone down in church history as wonderful servants of Jesus. Their names are recorded for eternity here in God's eternal Word. Church tradition states that most of those named here were martyred for their faith. Imagine dear sister Phoebe carrying with her a letter to Rome that contained the greatest wealth of Christian theology. A copy of that letter she carried is the letter you are now reading!

³Give my love[a] to Prisca and Aquila,[b] my partners in ministry serving the Anointed One, Jesus, ⁴for they've risked their own lives to save mine. I'm so thankful for them, and not just I, but all the congregations among the non-Jewish people respect them for their ministry. ⁵Also give my loving greetings to all the believers in their house church.

And greet Epenetus,[c] who was the first convert to Christ in the Roman province of Asia, for I love him dearly.[d]

⁶And give my greetings to Miriam,[e] who has toiled and labored extremely hard to beautify you.[f]

⁷Make sure that my relatives Andronicus and Junia[g] are honored, for they're my fellow captives[h] who bear the distinctive mark of being

---

a 16:3 The Aramaic word used throughout this chapter for "greetings" is "send peace."

b 16:3 Prisca was a diminutive form of Priscilla ("long life"). She and her husband, Aquila ("eagle"), were tentmakers like Paul. They were not only business partners, but partners with him in ministry. See Acts 18:2, 18, and 26, 1 Corinthians 16:19, and 2 Timothy 4:19.

c 16:5 Or "Epaenetus," which means "praiseworthy."

d 16:5 Or "the first fruit (convert) of Asia (Minor)." The Roman province of Asia is modern-day Turkey. The Aramaic has Epenetus as the first convert from Achaia, a region of Greece.

e 16:6 Or "Mary." The Hebrew name Miriam is taken from the Hebrew root and Ugaritic noun *mrym*, which means "height, summit, exalted (excellent)."

f 16:6 As translated from the Aramaic. The Greek is "to benefit you."

g 16:7 Throughout the first 1,200 years of church history, Andronicus ("victorious one") and Junia ("youthful") were considered to be husband and wife. A small number of manuscripts have "Julia." Paul calls them his relatives, or "(Jewish) kinsmen." The Aramaic meaning of Junia is "little dove."

h 16:7 Or "prisoners." It is possible that Paul is using this term as a metaphor; that is, they were prisoners of the love of Christ. See Song of Songs 8:6, which uses the Hebrew word for "prison cell" or "seal."

outstanding and well-known apostles,[a] and who were joined into the Anointed One before me.

[8]Give my regards to Ampliatus,[b] whom I love, for he is joined into the Lord.

[9]And give my loving greetings to Urbanus,[c] our partner in ministry serving the Anointed One, and also to Stachus,[d] whom I love.

[10]Don't forget to greet Apelles[e] for me, for he's been tested and found to be approved by the Anointed One.[f]

And extend warm greetings to all those of Aristobolos's house church.[g]

---

[a] 16:7 It is clear in the text that Junia, along with her husband, Andronicus, was a well-known apostle. (The Greek word *episemos* means "famous, prominent, outstanding.") Jesus chose twelve men and called them apostles, but the Twelve were not the only ones identified in the New Testament as apostles ("sent ones"). There are others, including Matthias, Paul, Barnabas, Andronicus, and Junia. See Acts 14:13 and Ephesians 4:11–13.

[b] 16:8 Ampliatus was a common name given to slaves, and it means "large one." The Eastern Orthodox Church recognizes him as one of the seventy disciples whom Jesus sent out. He is believed to have become the bishop of Bulgaria.

[c] 16:9 Urbanus was also a common name given to slaves. It means "polite one."

[d] 16:9 Or Stachys ("head of grain"). He is said to have been one of the seventy disciples Jesus sent out. He eventually became the bishop of Byzantium.

[e] 16:10 Apelles means "called one."

[f] 16:10 Or "the Lord knows, not we, the tests he endured."

[g] 16:10 Or "those of Aristobolos"; by implication, those connected to Aristobolos, or, his "house church." The word *household* is not found in the Greek text. Aristobolos means "best counselor." Traditionally he is known as one of the seventy disciples Jesus sent out, and he brought the gospel to Britain.

¹¹Give my love to my relative Herodian,ᵃ and also to all those of the house church of Narcissus,ᵇ for they too are joined into the Lord.

¹²Please greet Tryphenaᶜ and Tryphosa,ᵈ for they are women who have diligently served the Lord.

To Persis,ᵉ who is much loved and faithful in her ministry for the Lord, I send my greetings.

¹³And Rufus,ᶠ for he is especially chosen by the Lord. And I greet his mother, who was like a mother to me.

---

ᵃ 16:11 Herodian's name means "heroic." He was traditionally considered as one of Jesus' seventy disciples. He later became the bishop of Neoparthia (Iraq), where he was beaten to death by the Jews but was resurrected and continued to preach the gospel. It is believed that he was eventually beheaded in Rome on the same day Peter was martyred.

ᵇ 16:11 Or "those of Narcissus." Although nearly every translation adds the word *household*, it is not found in the text. By implication, this would be those meeting as a church in his house. Narcissus's name means "astonished (stupefied)." Some have identified him as a close friend of Emperor Claudius.

ᶜ 16:12 Tryphena means "living luxuriously." Some have identified her as Antonia Tryphaena (10 BC–AD 55), the princess of the Bosporan kingdom of eastern Crimea, and connected to the queen of Thrace. This would mean that she was royal and wealthy.

ᵈ 16:12 Tryphosa can also mean "living luxuriously" or "triple (three-fold) shining." Some scholars believe that Tryphena and Tryphosa were twin sisters born into royalty.

ᵉ 16:12 Persis means "to take by storm." She was a woman from Persia (Iranian background) who was a godly servant and passionate follower of Jesus.

ᶠ 16:13 Rufus means "red." It is believed that he was the son of Simon of Cyrene (Libya) who helped Jesus carry his cross to Calvary. See Mark 15:21.

¹⁴I cannot forget to mention my esteemed friends Asyncritus,ᵃ Phlegon,ᵇ Hermes,ᶜ Patrobas,ᵈ Hermas,ᵉ and all the brothers and sisters who meet with them.

¹⁵Give my regards to Philologus,ᶠ Julia, Nereus and his sister, and also Olympas and all the holy believers who meet with them.

---

ₐ 16:14 Asyncritus means "incomparable." The Orthodox Church recognizes him as an apostle. He became the bishop of the church of Hyracania (Turkey). In this verse Paul joins five men together. They could have represented the five-fold ministry of Ephesians 4:11, or they may have been leaders of house churches, for there were others who were "with" them and connected to them.

ᵇ 16:14 Phlegon means "burning one." He was considered to be one of the seventy disciples Jesus sent out. The Orthodox Church recognizes him as an apostle who became the bishop of Marathon in Thrace.

ᶜ 16:14 Hermes means "preacher of the deity." He was considered to be one of the seventy sent out by Jesus and later became the bishop of Dalmatia.

ᵈ 16:14 Patrobas means "fatherly (paternal)." He likewise was one of the seventy sent by Jesus and later became the bishop of Neapolis (Naples).

ₑ 16:14 Hermas was one of the seventy and later became the bishop of Philipopoulis (Bulgaria). There are interesting traditions surrounding Hermas. It is said that he was a very wealthy man but fell into poverty because of his sins. He was visited by an "angel of repentance," who accompanied him for the rest of his life until he was martyred. There are writings known as "The Shepherd of Hermas" that some scholars attribute to him.

ᶠ 16:15 Philologus means "talkative." He was recognized by the Orthodox Church as an apostle of Christ. It is likely that Julia was his wife and Nereus and his sister were their children. Olympas means "heavenly." The Orthodox Church recognizes Olympas as an apostle who was mentored by Peter and was beheaded the same day Peter was martyred in Rome. Philologus and Olympas apparently had a measure of influence over a number of "holy believers" in the faith. The majority of the people named in this chapter were not Jewish, and many of their names indicate that they were former slaves. God can bless and anoint anyone who turns to him in faith.

[16]Greet each other with a holy kiss *of God's love.*[a] All the believers in all the congregations of the Messiah send their greetings to all of you.

## Paul's Final Instructions

[17]And now, dear brothers and sisters, I'd like to give one final word of caution: Watch out for those who cause divisions and offenses among you. When they antagonize you by speaking of things that are contrary to the teachings that you've received, don't be caught in their snare! [18]For people like this are not truly serving the Lord, our Messiah, but are being driven by their own desires for a following.[b] Utilizing their smooth words and well-rehearsed blessings, they seek to deceive the hearts of innocent ones.

[19]I'm so happy when I think of you, because everyone knows the testimony of your deep commitment of faith. So I want you to become scholars of all that is good and beautiful, and stay pure and innocent[c] when it comes to evil. [20]And the God of peace will swiftly pound Satan to a pulp[d] under your feet! And the wonderful favor of our Lord Jesus will surround you.

---

a 16:16 What makes a kiss holy is that it comes from the love of God. See Song of Songs 1:2.

b 16:18 Or "They are slaves of their bellies." The metaphor used here is that they are driven by their desires to pull others into their group and thus divide the church.

c 16:19 Or "unmixed."

d 16:20 The Greek word *suntribo* means "to beat up someone to a jelly (pulp)." See also Psalm 60:12.

²¹My ministry partner, Timothy,ᵃ sends his loving greetings, along with Luke,ᵇ Jason,ᶜ and Sosipater,ᵈ my Jewish kinsmen.ᵉ

²²(I, Tertius,ᶠ am the one transcribing this letter for Paul, and I too send my greetings to all of you, as a follower of the Lord.)

²³My kind host here in Corinth, Gaius,ᵍ likewise greets you, along with the entire congregation of his house church. Also, the city administrator Erastusʰ and our brother Quartusⁱ send their warm greetings.

---

ₐ 16:21 Timothy was a spiritual son and ministry partner to the apostle Paul. See Acts 16:1–3.

ᵦ 16:21 Or "Lucius." This seems to be the Luke who wrote Luke and Acts, but there remains considerable debate surrounding who that "Luke" may be.

ᵪ 16:21 Jason also appears in Acts 17, where he opened his home to Paul, Silas, and Timothy while they were in Thessalonica. Tradition states that Jason was one of the seventy disciples sent out by Jesus and was appointed the bishop of Tarsus by Paul.

ₔ 16:21 According to church tradition, he was recognized as one of the seventy disciples and became the bishop of Iconium.

ₑ 16:21 See Acts 20:4.

ᵩ 16:22 Tertius, the copyist for Paul, was recognized in church history as one of the seventy disciples of Jesus. He became the bishop of Iconium after Sosipater and was eventually martyred.

ᵧ 16:23 This is most likely the Gaius whom Paul baptized (1 Corinthians 1:14) and who became a ministry partner with Paul (Acts 19:29). Gaius means "happy, jolly."

ₕ 16:23 Erastus was a political appointee who was undoubtedly of a high social status in the city of Corinth. His duties would have included being the treasurer of the city. Church tradition holds that he was one of the seventy disciples of Jesus and that he served as a minister (deacon) of the church in Jerusalem and later in Paneas. An excavation in Corinth uncovered a street with an ancient inscription dated to the first century AD. It read, "Erastus...laid the pavement at his own expense." His name means "loveable."

ᵢ 16:23 Quartus is recognized in church history as one of the seventy disciples sent by Jesus. He become the bishop of Beirut. Nikolai Velimirovic wrote that Quartus suffered greatly for his faith and won many converts to Christ through his ministry (*Prologue from Ohrid*).

[24]May the grace and favor of our Lord Jesus, the Anointed One, continually rest upon you all.[a]

## Paul Praises God

[25]I give all my praises and glory[b] to the one who has more than enough power to make you strong and keep you steadfast through the promises found in the wonderful news that I preach; that is, the proclamation of Jesus, the Anointed One. This wonderful news includes the unveiling of the mystery kept secret[c] from the dawn of creation until now. [26]This mystery is understood through the prophecies of the Scripture and by the decree of the eternal God. And it is now heard openly by all the nations, igniting within them a deep commitment of faith.

[27]Now to God, the only source of wisdom, be glorious praises for endless ages through Jesus, the Anointed One! Amen!

(Paul's letter was transcribed by Tertius in Corinth and sent from Corinth and carried to Rome by Phoebe.)

---

a  16:24 The vast majority of Greek manuscripts have verse 24; however, some manuscripts, including the Aramaic, place this verse after verse 27. There is some external evidence that this verse was copied from verse 20 and placed here. Many scholars are divided over where or if this verse is to be placed in the text.

b  16:25 Implied in the text and supplied from verse 27 for the sake of English sentence length. This doxology of Paul (vv. 25–27) is found in three separate locations in different Greek manuscripts with a total of five variations. Most reliable manuscripts place it here. Some have it after 14:23, and a few place it after 15:33. Some include it twice in different placements.

c  16:25 Or "kept in (God's) silence."

# About the Translator

Dr. Brian Simmons is known as a passionate lover of God. After a dramatic conversion to Christ, Brian knew that God was calling him to go to the unreached people of the world and present the gospel of God's grace to all who would listen. With his wife, Candice, and their three children, he spent nearly eight years in the tropical rain forest of the Darien Province of Panama as a church planter, translator, and consultant. Brian was involved in the Paya-Kuna New Testament translation project. He studied linguistics and Bible translation principles with New Tribes Mission. After their ministry in the jungle, Brian was instrumental in planting a thriving church in New England (USA), and now travels full time as a speaker and Bible teacher. He has been happily married to Candice for over forty-two years and is known to boast regularly of his children and grandchildren. Brian and Candice may be contacted at:

## Facebook.com/passiontranslation
## Twitter.com/tPtBible

For more information about the translation project or any of Brian's books, please visit:

## thePassionTranslation.com
## StairwayMinistries.org

Dr. David Jeremiah.
Notes Turning Point
9-5

More than Conquerors Rom 8-37-
Whatever is going on in my
life God is greater, We are over-
comers, He gives us the strength
to overcome. V 38-
Song - Oh love that will not let
me go.

Turning Points The Love God which is in Christ
9-5 not the Cries of death. nor the Jesus
Calamities of life
B. not the intervention of angles
nor intervention of demons.
angels report to God.
                    Cares
not the Concerns of the day
or the Concerns of tomorrow.
nor anything in all Creation.
When we are in the deepest need
He comes to me, He has me in
his hands
Luther a mighty Fortress is
our God.

# Notes

# Notes

# Notes

# Notes

# Notes

# Notes

# Notes

# Notes

# Notes

# Notes

# Notes

# Notes

thePassionTranslation.com